Schrag

March 1975 $2

To Jake
Christmas, 1974
from Florence

Divorce and Remarriage

A Perspective for Counseling

Divorce and Remarriage

A Perspective for Counseling

John R. Martin

Herald Press, Scottdale, Pennsylvania
1974

Library of Congress Cataloging in Publication Data

Martin, John R 1928-
   Divorce and remarriage.

   Originally presented as the author's thesis (Th.M.)
Eastern Baptist Theological Seminary, 1972.
   Bibliography: p. 132
   1. Marriage. 2. Divorce. 3. Remarriage.
4. Pastoral counseling. I. Title.
BV835.M25 1974   253.5   73-18038
ISBN O-8361-1729-8

DIVORCE AND REMARRIAGE: A PERSPECTIVE FOR COUNSELING
Copyright © 1974 by Herald Press, Scottdale, Pennsylvania 15683
Library of Congress Catalog Card Number: 73-18038
International Standard Book Number: 0-8361-1729-8
Printed in the United States of America

To my wife, Marian,
And to my children,
Don, Lee, and Ann,
Who provide a genuine home base
From which I can reach out to others.

Preface

The following pages explore how a pastor with convictions regarding the permanence of marriage can effectively counsel persons considering divorce or remarriage. Since a counselor's attitudes on moral and social issues frequently determine how he relates to persons involved in these issues, a pastor-counselor needs to clarify his own theological and professional understandings. One purpose of this book is to provide this needed understanding.

A second purpose is to give guidance in receiving as church members persons who have been divorced and remarried. This matter is not given major attention but it is discussed at several points.

Increasingly our pastors are becoming counselors to members and nonmembers who are contemplating divorce or remarriage. The number of crumbling marriages and broken homes is rising within our congregations as is the pattern in society in general. Pastors who are strongly oriented in Mennonite practices of the past generation find it difficult to counsel effectively in these situations.

Pastors with training in counseling frequently find a conflict between their biblical understanding of divorce and remarriage and the current sociological and psychological approach to these issues. The problem is that of dealing redemptively with persons caught in irretrievable marriage and divorce and at the same time being true to a high view of marriage.

The traditional approach is inadequate because it does not serve the current needs of persons caught in problem marriages and divorce. I believe that an alternative to the traditional approach can be found which will provide a workable solution for these persons based on both the biblical view of the marriage commitment and the dynamics of their individual situations. I believe that persons who have been divorced and remarried may be received as church members on an individual basis when it is evident that forgiveness and faith have been personalized in their lives and marriage relationships.

My approach in this book involves a study of biblical and historical material regarding marriage, divorce, and remarriage, a study of the dynamics of marriage and divorce, and a study of basic counseling methodology. Resources include case studies and personal pastoral experiences.

The book is divided into two major parts. The first, dealing with counseling perspectives, presents background material designed to give the counselor a clearer perspective concerning divorce and remarriage. Perhaps the greatest need is "educating" the pastor.

The first chapter focuses on the biblical teachings regarding divorce and remarriage. It encompasses a summary of the Old Testament and New Testament points of view, a summary of approaches used by various Christian churches, an examination of the essence of marriage, and finally a review of the positions held by the Mennonite Church during its history along with a statement of contemporary understanding.

Chapter 2 goes behind the scenes and attempts to understand why so many marriages are failing. This is valuable in understanding what may be bringing the couple to the brink of divorce.

Chapter 3 highlights the painful road of divorce. At a time when couples in conflict are looking for an easy out, the counselor needs to be able to bring a dimension of realism to their thinking.

Part II focuses on how the pastor goes about the task of counseling. The concern is methodology. The first chapter of this section presents some guidelines for counseling and the next chapter applies these principles in counseling persons considering divorce. The final chapter applies the same principles in counseling persons considering remarriage. Both chapters 2 and 3 of Part II include a case study to give a feel of reality to the procedure.

In the past decade or two, numerous studies have been made and papers written regarding the biblical attitude toward divorce and remarriage and whether we should receive such persons into church fellowship. One of the most helpful resources is the booklet by J. C. Wenger, *Dealing Redemptively with Those Involved in Divorce and Remarriage Problems*. However, none of these studies, to my knowledge, were approached from a counseling perspective. It is this additional dimension that I feel is needed today.

The material in this book was originally prepared as a Master's thesis at Eastern Baptist Theological Seminary. I am especially indebted to Dr. William J. Hand for his stimulation in the classroom and his helpful guidance in planning for the thesis.

I am also indebted to Myron Ebersole, my clinical supervisor at Lancaster General Hospital, for his suggestions involving background studies. Further, I am indebted to many pastors and lay members for their enrichment of my understandings in known and unknown ways.

A special word of appreciation is due my wife, Marian, for her encouragement in the task and for typing the manuscript.

Certainly this book is not the last word on the complex problem of counseling persons considering divorce or remarriage. But it does represent growth in my understanding. If it proves to be helpful to others, my prayer and desire for it are fulfilled.

John R. Martin

Introduction

The American home is in trouble. The causes for the illness or even breakdown of many marriages are undoubtedly complex and baffling. But here is a helpful book by a pastor and scholar who wants to be wholly faithful to Christ, who deplores marriage failure and divorce, and yet who wishes to help those involved in these painful situations.

The author is earnestly seeking for the will of God as set forth in His Word, especially by our Lord and His Spirit-filled apostles. He wants to discover how to save as many marriages as possible. He wants to explore a redemptive program for those whose marriages have failed. He wants to manifest the same accepting love and concern as did the Lord when dealing with an oft-married woman of Samaria. Regardless of what our convictions on these matters may be, we owe it to those we are seeking to help to consider seriously the insights presented here.

The most valuable facet of this book is the fact that the author does not opt for an extreme position, either to gloss over the tragedy of divorce or to treat it as an unpardonable sin. What he does endeavor to do is to find a position which holds to the permanent character of marriage in God's intention, and which at the same time offers loving acceptance to broken persons regardless of where they are in the marriage/divorce/remarriage spectrum.

Pastors and other counselors will find the case studies, and the interpretative comments on them, both helpful and illuminating. Here we see fallible humans functioning, to be sure, but we also see concerned counselors discerning the best possible approach to bring the will of God to bear on each situation. The author does not claim to have easy and simplistic answers, but he does give evidence of relating in the love of the Spirit to those who desperately need the grace of God as they try to discover the way of faithful obedience to Christ.

Christ's church owes a debt of gratitude to John R. Martin for the courage to face these difficult questions, and to stand without apology for a position which he sees as that of faithfulness to our Lord and Master Jesus Christ.

J. C. Wenger
Goshen, Indiana
March 28, 1973

Contents

Preface 7

Introduction by J. C. Wenger 11

Part I. COUNSELING PERSPECTIVES

1. Biblical Teachings Regarding Divorce and
   Remarriage 17

   Old Testament and New Testament Summary
   Attitudes of the Christian Church Toward Divorce
     and Remarriage
   Basic Understandings of Marriage, Divorce, and
     Remarriage
   A Mennonite Understanding of Marriage, Divorce,
     and Remarriage

2. Why Do Marriages Fail? 41

   Forces Destroying Marriages
   Requirements for Successful Marriage

3. Is Divorce the Answer? 59

   The Emotional Cost of Divorce
   The Futility of Divorce

Part II. COUNSELING PROCEDURES

1. A Model for Pastoral Counseling   73

2. Counseling Persons Considering Divorce   87

   Case Study
   Assess the Marriage
   Examine the Options
   Pastoral Care During and Following Divorce

3. Counseling Persons Considering Remarriage 111

   Case Study
   Face Past Failures
   Assess Present Maturity
   Examine Future Implications

4. Conclusion 127

Bibliography 132

Index 134

Part I

COUNSELING PERSPECTIVES

Biblical Teachings Regarding Divorce and Remarriage

Since the beginning of the Mennonite Church in 1525, Mennonites have been biblicists in the best sense of the term. They have not viewed the Bible as a "wooden pope," but rather God's inspired revelation to man or God's Word written. For them it is authoritative in faith and life. It is understandable then that the first consideration in ethical matters is, "What say the Scriptures?" This section will present in summary form the teachings of the Scriptures regarding divorce and remarriage as well as the various ways in which these teachings have been interpreted by the Christian church and the Mennonite brotherhood.

Old Testament and New Testament Summary

It seems apparent that the practice of divorce is taken for granted in the Old Testament. There were no laws justifying the practice; rather, it related to man's privileged position. The key passage for understanding divorce in the Old Testament, Deuteronomy 24:1-4, assumes man's privilege of divorce. However, certain restrictions are placed on man primarily for the protection of the woman. (See also Jeremiah 3:1.)

The primary intent of the Deuteronomic passage is obscured in the King James Version. Verse 1 implies it is the will of God for a man to divorce his wife if he finds in her something offensive. A correct rendering of the Hebrew runs the if clause to the end of verse 3. Observe the three uses of "if."

When a man takes a wife and marries her, if then she finds no favor in his eyes because he has found some indecency in her, and he writes her a bill of divorce and puts it in her hand and sends her out of his house, and she departs out of his house, and if she goes and becomes another man's wife, and the latter husband dislikes her and writes her a bill of divorce and puts it in her hand and sends her out of his house, or if the latter husband dies, who took her to be his wife, then her former husband, who sent her away, may not take her again to be his wife, after she has been defiled; for that is an abomination before the Lord, and you shall not bring guilt upon the land which the Lord your God gives you for an inheritance. Deuteronomy 24: 1-4.

God recognized that Israel in her sinful condition would divorce and remarry. But the resuming of a marriage after a second marriage had been consummated was absolutely forbidden. It mattered not whether the second marriage ended in divorce or by the death of the second husband. Commenting on this passage, J. C. Wenger says that "God tolerates divorce in this passage, but does not institute or command it. What God does do, is to forbid the resumption of a union which has been broken by a second marriage." [1]

In interpreting this same passage, William Cole notes that "a man must have good cause to put away his wife, that he must go before a public official and set forth his grounds, which must then be written out in an official document and given to the woman. All of this mitigated against hasty and unconsidered action." [2] It should also be noted that the initiative lay completely in the hands of the husband. The wife, apparently, could not initiate divorce.

Other Old Testament teachings carry the same concern of protection for the woman. If a man seduced a girl and was forced to marry her, he could not put her away. Deuteronomy 22 states this prohibition.

If a man meets a virgin who is not betrothed, and seizes her and lies with her, and they are found, then the man who lay with her shall give to the father of the young woman fifty shekels of silver, and she shall be his wife, because he violated her; he may not put her away all his days. Deuteronomy 22:28, 29. (See also verses 13-19.)

In spite of this prohibition, divorce was practiced freely. But there are evidences indicating Israel knew divorce was below God's intention. The message of Malachi is one example.

And this again you do. You cover the Lord's altar with tears, with weeping and groaning because he no longer regards the offering or accepts it with favor at your hand. You ask, "Why does he not?" Because the Lord was witness to the covenant between you and the wife of your youth, to whom you have been faithless, though she is your companion and your wife by covenant. Has not the one God made and sustained for us the spirit of life? And what does he desire? Godly offspring. So take heed to yourselves, and let none be faithless to the wife of his youth. "For I hate divorce, says the Lord the God of Israel, and covering one's garment with violence, says the Lord of hosts. So take heed to yourselves and do not be faithless." Malachi 2:13-16.

In summary we notice (1) that divorce and remarriage was practiced in Israel, (2) that while there were no laws forbidding divorce and remarriage, the practice was displeasing to God, and (3) that resuming a marriage following a second marriage was strictly forbidden.

The key New Testament passage relating to divorce and remarriage is Mark 10:2-12 with parallels in Matthew 19:1-9 and Luke 16:18. The focus of Christ's teaching was in response to the questions of the Pharisees.

And Pharisees came up and in order to test him asked, "Is it lawful for a man to divorce his wife?" He answered them, "What did Moses command you?" They said, "Moses allowed a man to write a certificate of divorce, and to put her away." But Jesus said to them, "For your hardness of heart he wrote you this commandment. But from the beginning of creation, 'God made them male and female.' 'For this reason a man shall leave his father and mother and be joined to his wife, and the two shall become one flesh.' So they are no longer two but one flesh. What therefore God has joined together, let not man put asunder."

And in the house the disciples asked him again about this matter. And he said to them, "Whoever divorces his wife and marries another, commits adultery against her; and if she divorces her husband and marries another, she commits adultery." Mark 10:2-12.

The teachings of Christ and the apostles pass over the directives in Deuteronomy and go back to Genesis 1 and 2. They see in this foundational teaching God's will that marriage be the union of one man and one woman for life. Christ clearly rejected the easy divorce pattern Israel was following and called them back to the original plan given at Creation to Adam and Eve.

Some see in the Pharisees' question an attempt to clarify a conflict between conservative rabbinical scholars under the leadership of Shammai, who interpreted the "indecency" of Deuteronomy 24:1 to mean only adultery, and the liberal rabbinical scholars under the leadership of Hillel, who interpreted it to mean any cause, even burning a meal. Christ in His reply rejected both of these interpretations as being God's original plan or as being God's plan for His day. The Apostle Paul confirms the same position in Romans 7 and 1 Corinthians 7. Marriage is to be permanent and divorce is no longer allowed.

A possible exception to this absolute position is found in chapters 5 and 19 of Matthew. What did Christ mean by the exception clause? Cole says, "Many New Testament scholars regard Matthew's addition as much later, edited by someone seeking to soften a too harsh dictum." [3] Thielicke questions whether they are additions. In my opinion the textual problem does not seem significant enough to ignore Matthew's teachings.

But what did Christ actually say in Matthew 5:32? Regarding divorce He said, "every one who divorces his wife, except on the ground of unchastity, makes her an adulteress." How? By putting her in a situation where she will likely marry another man while in God's sight her union with her first husband still stands; hence, adultery. If, however, a wife has been unfaithful and this becomes the reason for the divorce, the husband is not guilty of making her an adulteress because she has already become this by her unfaithfulness.

It should be noted that the exception clause in no way *commands* a man to divorce his unfaithful wife. Such an interpretation would be inconsistent with the total teaching of Scripture. Also, it should be observed that Christ is not merely referring to premarital unchastity. The term translated "fornication" in the New Testament is used to refer to sexual sins of both single and married people.

Matthew 19:9 has a slightly different thrust, namely, the sin of illicit remarriage. The central message is "whoever divorces . . . and marries another, commits adultery." The exception clause, "except for unchastity," seems to imply that the unchastity of the wife releases the husband from the marriage bond. J. C. Wenger, commenting on this Scripture, says, "The sin of contracting a union with someone other than one's spouse is so awful that it has the same effect on the marriage bond as does death. The innocent party may remarry without sin. This is the implication of the grammar. But it should be noted that this conclusion is never explicitly stated anywhere in the New Testament." [4] The Apostle Paul is apparently expressing a similar truth in 1 Corinthians 6: 15-18. It should also be noted that the Scriptures do not consider it sinful for a marriage to continue even though one party of the marriage is unfaithful.

In Paul's discussion of marriage in 1 Corinthians 7, several significant truths should be noted. First, if a Christian couple experiences such severe incompatibility that they decide on separation, they shall remain unmarried or effect a reconciliation (vv. 10 and 11). Second, if one member of a pagan couple becomes a believer and there is conflict between Christianity and paganism, the believer shall let the unbeliever depart. In this situation the Christian partner "is not bound" (v. 15). Many see Paul setting forth irremedial desertion as a valid ground for terminating the marriage bond.

One very disturbing question relates to whether continuing in a second marriage with a former companion still living, constitutes a continuing sin of adultery. J. C. Wenger answers this question in the following way:

> The question of whether adultery is a state or an act compares somewhat with the matter of being married to an unbeliever. Surely that is a state, not just an initial situation when the marriage began. And for a Christian to marry an unbeliever is clearly a sin by New Testament standards. Yet we recall at once the New Testament permission, yea even counsel, to continue such unions with non-Christians where the unbeliever is willing. Does this imply the right of divorced people to continue their union even when sinfully contracted in the first place? [5]

In a study paper presented by Howard H. Charles on "Some Aspects of the New Testament Teaching on Divorce and Remarriage," he deals as follows with the question of whether adultery is a state or an act:

> Is a married couple one of whom has been previously divorced for unscriptural reasons living in a state of adultery? To be sure, they are guilty of adultery. The consummation of the second marriage was an act of adultery against the previous marriage but it was also an act which destroyed the validity of that marriage. Where the sin that destroyed the first marriage in the inauguration of the second union has been adequately dealt with it would appear that the second union could be continued without fresh guilt being incurred daily as these two people live to-

gether. It must be admitted that this explanation is not a "thus saith the Lord," and where the Christian conscience can find no rest in this solution the only alternative is to discontinue a relationship which to them is sinful. In any case it may be noted that the expression "living in adultery," which we sometimes use, is not found in the New Testament. [6]

The New Testament teachings on divorce and remarriage, plus remaining questions, may be summarized as follows:

1. The intention of God regarding the permanence of marriage is best expressed in His teachings in Genesis 1 and 2, not in the practice of Israel. It is God's intention that marriage be the union of one man and one woman for life. Mark and Luke state the general principle and Matthew mentions a possible exception.

2. While a possible exception is mentioned in Matthew 5 and 19 where there is unchastity, some deep problems still remain. Matthew 5:32 implies that divorce, at least where there has not been unchastity, does not dissolve the marriage union. But if unchastity does dissolve the marriage union, as is suggested in Matthew 19:9 and implied by both Wenger and Charles; then why didn't Christ command couples to divorce when unchastity takes place? Furthermore, the concept of a truly "innocent party" in a marriage breakdown is highly questionable.

3. Paul, in 1 Corinthians 7, recognizes the possibility of severe incompatibility in a Christian marriage and a resulting separation. However, in such a case, they shall either remain unmarried or effect a reconciliation. But when an unbeliever chooses to dissolve a marriage relation with a believer the believer "is not bound" to continue the marriage relation and can presumably remarry. Does Paul assume the nature of marriage for the Christian and non-Christian are different? Paul does not attempt to answer this question.

4. It appears that the New Testament regards adultery as an act rather than a state. Therefore, a second marriage,

while the partner of the first marriage is still living, can be free from continual sin where there has been sincere repentance and the claiming of forgiveness.

Attitudes of the Christian Church Toward Divorce and Remarriage

The problem of understanding the biblical teachings on divorce and remarriage is complicated by the various interpretations of Scripture adopted by the Christian church. The variety of interpretations reflect not so much the question, What do the Scriptures say? but rather, What do the Scriptures mean? The answer to this latter question becomes more and more diverse. But it is important to become familiar with this diversity.

Among the various summaries that have been made, I find Wayne E. Oates in his book *Pastoral Counseling in Social Problems* to be most helpful. Oates summarizes the attitudes of the Christian church toward divorce and remarriage under four basic approaches.

1. The Laissez-Faire Approach

This approach is expressed in several ways, one of which is the "marrying parson" who agrees to marry any couple requesting his services. He likely sees some magical blessing in marriage by a minister and rationalizes that they will marry anyway even if he refuses to perform the ceremony. The "marrying parson" has little concern about the possible degree of success or failure of the marriage. His services are simply available to all who want to be married.

Another expression of the laissez-faire approach is the legalist who says he will have nothing to do with any divorced person. He only ministers to divorced persons by telling them he is not open to providing any ministry to divorced persons. He has an institutionally oriented ministry rather than a pastorally oriented ministry.

Reflecting on this approach and various ways it is expressed one can see struggling pastors caught in a narrow bind. Either they are ignorant of the causes and unique problems related to divorce or they do not understand the deep personal needs of the divorcee. In either case, the approach is basically the same, namely, I will do anything asked of me by a divorced person seeking remarriage or I will do nothing asked of me by a divorced person seeking remarriage. Obviously the pattern of Christ's ministry and the biblical understanding of people and marriage are being completely overlooked.

2. *The Idealistic Approach*

Churches and pastors taking this approach say that the Christian ideal makes no provision for remarriage of divorcees, ruling out any justification on the basis of the "saving clause" or adultery.

The Acts of Convocation in the Anglican Church at the Convocation of Canterbury in its regulations concerning marriage and divorce states this position quite clearly. It sees the marriage union dissoluble only by death. Remarriage during the lifetime of a former partner is always a departure from Christ's teaching. The church upholds the principle of lifelong obligation in marriage by refusing to perform any marriage while a former partner is still living.

In the eyes of some this position is not merely an ideal but an honest recognition of what marriage is by its very nature. Some holding this view still take seriously the pastoral care and rehabilitation of the remarried person even though they do not perform public weddings for such persons. The Convocation of Canterbury describes such a procedure. The pastor counsels with the couple seeking marriage. Pertinent information about the couple is given to the bishop for his evaluation. If he feels the couple is living in good faith with the church, the marriage is approved. The

25

couple is then married by the civil authorities and the church recognizes the validity of the marriage. They may even provide "a service of blessing" but they attempt to keep the biblical standard clear by refraining from performing the marriage ceremony.

The assumption that there are no valid grounds for justifying remarriage is based on both psychological and theological understandings. People sometimes refer to the partner who did not fall morally as "innocent." But to assume there can be an "innocent party" ignores the broken relationship which motivates a spouse to "commit adultery." Unfaithfulness is an expression of a sick marriage, not its cause. Furthermore, to call one party "innocent" and one "guilty" is to ignore the fact that all have sinned.

In favor of the idealistic approach is the attempt to be both true to God's intention for marriage and sensitive to the human situations of sinful persons. However, the questions still remain: What does Christ mean by the "exception clause" in Matthew 5 and 19? If the church will "approve" a marriage, why can its representatives not perform the ceremony?

3. The Forensic Approach

The forensic approach sees the teachings of Christ regarding remarriage as applicable to Christian marriage but not marriage in general. The Roman Catholic Church follows this approach in dealing with the problem of remarriage by viewing marriage as a sacrament for those who are baptized. The church sits in judgment on the first marriage to determine whether it was a true Christian marriage; hence, the term *forensic* approach.

Several basic questions are raised by the church. Was the previous marriage of the person seeking remarriage a Christian marriage? Were they professing Christians and members of the church? Since the divorce, have the parties become Christians? Is every effort being made to make the new marriage Christian?

The concern in this approach is to determine the theological condition of the previous marriage and to prepare the couple for a true marriage in the remarriage. It keeps the doctrine of redemption above the doctrine of divorce. However, it seems to limit true marriage to a covenant between Christians.

The recent position adopted by some sections of the Mennonite Church is similar to this approach in that it permits receiving as members persons who experienced divorce and remarriage prior to conversion. However, the reason is not that the first marriage was invalid, but rather that Christ brings forgiveness for all past sins at conversion and the convert should continue to live in the marriage relationship where he happened to be at that time (1 Corinthians 7).

The central question relating to this approach is whether true marriage is limited to Christians only. The New Testament seems to assume the marriage of non-Christians is valid, for it does not require a Christian ceremony for converted pagan couples. If pagan marriage were not valid, would not converted couples need a Christian marriage so they would not continue living in sin? The value of this approach is that it keeps the doctrine of redemption above the doctrine of divorce, but is not this possible without a sacramental view of marriage?

4. The Confrontational and Therapeutic Approach

In this approach, divorcees seeking remarriage are confronted with the claims of the Christian gospel and their own part in the failure of the previous marriage. Little effort is made to determine whether they were the guilty or innocent party, for all have sinned. Everyone involved in a divorce is responsible. Both spouses must face their share of guilt and even the church may share corporately in the sin. It shares in inadequate preparation for marriage, failure to provide adequate pastoral follow-up, and the loss of rapport when separation developed. The church attempts to be redemptive by putting forth every effort to provide a healing ministry where there are still hurts, a counseling ministry where guidance is needed, and a nurturing ministry where maturity is needed. If the couple will enter this level of relationship with the church, they will likely be able to enter a deep level of relationships with one another. The church then treats divorced persons similar to the way it treats the non-divorced. It marries only those who evidence a responsible commitment to the Christian faith.

In favor of this approach is an attempt to deal realistically with the past. The divorce represents failure and guilt. Complete innocence is not possible. Therefore, the past must be faced with repentance and forgiveness claimed. The present is also faced realistically. Persons who have experienced divorce face many spiritual, social, and emotional needs. The healing ministry of the church is urgently needed. But there is also a future that must be faced. The church is responsible to marry "only in the Lord." Is the couple living in Christian faith? Are they sufficiently mature to establish a sound relationship? These questions must be answered before the church can conscientiously perform the marriage ceremony.

This section has outlined four approaches of various churches and pastors to divorce and remarriage: willingness to marry (1) any couple who request it, (2) no divorced persons, (3) only Christians, and (4) those who examine their marriage commitment in relation to the claims of the gospel. These vary according to one's understanding of marriage and the Scriptures.

Basic Understandings of Marriage, Divorce, and Remarriage

After examining the four attitudes of the Christian church toward divorce and remarriage, it becomes evident that one's position on divorce and remarriage is determined by and grows out of one's understanding of marriage. This is to be expected because without marriage there could be no divorce and a major concern in remarriage is the previous marriage.

There are at least three basic approaches to marriage. It is difficult to find each approach in its pure form because there is frequently some overlap; however, there do appear to be three points of focus in looking at marriage, and the uniqueness of each focus is reflected in the attitude toward divorce and remarriage.

1. Sexual Union

The first approach sees the heart of marriage as sexual union. Viewed from one perspective, this is the biblical point of view. Marriage is presented as a relationship of trust and promise culminating in sexual union. In the Old Testament, this is illustrated in the marriage of Isaac and Rebekah. "Then Isaac brought her into the tent, and took Rebekah, and she became his wife; and he loved her" (Genesis 24:67). It is further illustrated in the law of Moses. Deuteronomy 22 says that a fornicator is compelled to marry the humiliated girl and gave him no license to put her away all her days. Menno Simons felt this law was still in force.

Piper sees this aspect of marriage as being basic to the concept that the two "become one flesh" (Genesis 2:24). He sees sexual union establishing a lasting bond between the two persons involved. It creates an inner union or "unity of the flesh," because it involves the wills of the persons.

29

It is a profoundly unique union that cannot be dissolved. It is an exclusive possession that cannot be shared with a third party. Piper describes the nature of the union as follows:

> Nevertheless, the unity established by the sexual relationship is not simply a momentary subjective experience, it is an objective and indelible feature of our Self which we cannot get rid of again. This is the reason why Jesus frowns upon divorce (Mark 10:2-12; Matthew 19:3-9). His rigorism would be meaningless if that union were nothing but an emotional or legal tie. Paul uses the same argument in order to show that a Christian must not have intercourse with prostitutes (1 Corinthians 6:16-20). Paul refutes the frivolous conception that sexual relationships are but fleeting and transient affairs of the body. A sexual experience is not only existential, being related to one's Self, but also brings about an ontic connection with the partner.[7]

If sexual union culminates the marriage, adultery then "breaks" the marriage union. Unfaithfulness becomes grounds for divorce. The "innocent" party is no longer bound to the "guilty" party who by his unfaithfulness broke the marriage union. The "innocent" party is free to divorce. This seems to be what Christ is saying in Matthew 5:32. The Mennonite attitude in the latter nineteenth century and the forensic approach reflect this point of view.

2. Covenant

A second approach to marriage looks at marriage in terms of covenant. It sees the heart or essence of marriage as being the vows. A couple promises one another and God to join lives until separated by death. The vows are made without qualifications or conditions. The ideal approach to marriage is reflected in this view.

Commenting on the biblical understanding of covenant, G. Ernest Wright points out the uniqueness of God's covenant with Israel. It combines personal responsibility to God and involvement in God's new community. It is described as "a responsibility which was without qualification or condition, which rested on the necessity of a complete and undeviating loyalty to the Lord . . . which arose not from legal necessity but from personal commitment." [8]

Perhaps the exchanging of marriage vows in the context of the worshiping community carries a similar understanding of the two dimensions of covenant. Furthermore, Wright suggests that sin "involved both rebellion against the Lord and violation of a community."[9] Therefore, the breaking of marriage vows should likewise be seen in this dual aspect.

The marriage covenant is made with full awareness of its unconditional nature. It is much more than an expression of intention, it is a pledge of promise until death. Its significance is seen in the fact of its being a covenant between a man and a woman and God. The marriage covenant is linked to God's covenant to man. Gibson Winter explains the connection in this way:

> There is a twofold link between God's covenant with His people and the covenant of marriage. First, God has created marriage for man and bestows His blessings upon it. This means that God promises to support and empower the covenant between husband and wife. . . . Second, the covenant of marriage is included in the broader covenant of God with His people. Marriage is not to be a substitute for faithfulness to God and membership in His people. . . . The covenant of intimacy is fulfilled in obedience to God and leads men more deeply into trust in God. If marriage becomes divorced from this broader covenant, it ceases to be a covenant relationship in the full meaning of the term. There can be contracts between men and women which they make and unmake. A covenant, however, is a unique relationship made before God and empowered by God.[10]

Since the covenant is totally unconditional, there are no grounds on which a spouse is free to divorce. They covenant to each other and God to be loving and faithful in plenty and in want, in joy and in sorrow, in sickness and in health so long as they both shall live.

Furthermore, remarriage is never permissible in this view as long as the first spouse is still living. To remarry would be to live in continual sin because the first marriage is still the valid one until the death of the partner. The Roman Catholic view sounds similar although they add a sacramental element to the marriage experience.

3. *Relational*

This approach to marriage focuses primarily on the relational aspect of life. Much of the current writing regarding marriage expresses this point of view. It is frequently the basic view of those who have a psychological orientation to life and may or may not include the concept of Christian covenant. The primary concern when considering marriage is how the couple relate.

Compatibility is the key word. Sexual compatibility is often viewed as an indication of the nature of their relationship. Sexual union is not necessarily the culmination of marriage. The vows may be seen as intention rather than covenant. Today's youth culture would take this approach to its extreme. For some youth the pattern of a formal marriage ceremony is outdated. If they relate well to one another and want to share life, at least for a while, they simply start living together.

For some the relational approach is taking the form of the communal family. Toffler envisions the possibility of "The banding together of several adults and children into a single 'family.' . . ."[11] Novelist Robert Rimmer has proposed that the possibility of a "corporate family" be legalized. Such a family would have three to six adults who would adopt a common name and raise children in common.

Another expression of the relational concept of marriage is the approach of temporary marriage. In such an arrangement, marriage continues as long as interpersonal relationships are mutually satisfactory. When they move beyond this point, the relationship is terminated and a new relationship is explored. Two of the persons promoting this pattern are the German theologian Siegfried Keil, who urges "recognized premarriage," and Father Jacques Lazure from Canada, who proposes "probationary marriages" of three to eighteen months.

When marriage is understood primarily on the relational level, divorce can be viewed as the dissolving of a relationship rather than the breaking of a covenant. If the relationship between spouses breaks down, it is terminated formally for those who have married and informally for those who are simply living together.

Remarriage then is simply entering a new relationship. It is approached basically as the first relationship was approached.

Which of these three understandings of marriage, divorce, and remarriage represents the Christian view? I believe that Christian marriage represents a combination of all three of these approaches to marriage. To focus on one aspect and ignore the others is to have a partial view of marriage and faulty conclusions regarding divorce and remarriage.

Specifically, this means that sexual union is very significant in marriage. The testimony of both the Old and New Testament is clear and united in this regard. In no way can sexual intercourse be justified before marriage nor can unfaithfulness be sanctioned within marriage. The sex act is a significant part of marriage, culminating the marriage union following the exchanging of the vows.

Covenant stands at the very heart of marriage. The Old Testament covenant made Israel God's unique possession. When Israel disobeyed God, the basic sin was not the act of disobedience but the breaking of covenant. Likewise in

Christian marriage, the covenant between husband and wife creates a unique sense of possession and belonging. Since it involves man, woman, and God, any breaking of the covenant is a sin against both the earthly and the heavenly partner in the marriage.

The relationship in which the couple lives is extremely important. Current writings in the field of marriage emphasize this strongly. It is also the concern of the Apostle Paul's discussion in Ephesians 5. He illustrates the relationship between Christ and the church by drawing a parallel to the relationship between husband and wife. The passage also indicates that the husband-wife relationship and the wife-husband relationship is to have the qualities of the Christ-church and the church-Christ relationships. Couples need premarital counseling to guide them in entering such a relationship. They need to understand that the quality of their marriage will be the sum total of their lives. Both will share in their success or in their failure.

A Mennonite Understanding of Marriage, Divorce, and Remarriage

The approach to this discussion will be primarily historical. How has the Mennonite brotherhood understood these aspects of human life and experience? Since the understanding of marriage has not varied significantly during the years, it will receive a brief discussion. Major attention will be given to the understanding of divorce and remarriage because the position has not been uniform throughout our history.

Mennonites have, since their beginning, based their understanding of marriage entirely on the New Testament. Menno Simons, an early Frisian leader, describes this understanding in the following words: "We acknowledge, teach, and assent to no other marriage than that which Christ and His apostles publicly and plainly taught in the

New Testament, namely, one man and one woman (Matthew 19:4), and that they may not be divorced except in case of adultery (Matthew 5:32); for the two are one flesh, but if the unbelieving one depart, a sister or brother is not under bondage in that case. 1 Corinthians 7:15."[12]

The strong emphasis on separation from the world soon led to the pattern of marrying only within the brotherhood. Marriages were performed in the presence of the congregation by authorized ministers but only after the couple had been examined. Emphasis on strict obedience to Christ strengthened the moral character of marriage. The consecrated view of life did away with the sacramental concept of marriage. Today marriage is not restricted to members of the brotherhood, but members are to marry only "in the Lord."

The Mennonite understanding of divorce and remarriage is more difficult to summarize. In 1527, two years after the beginning of the Anabaptist movement, a tract written by the Swiss Brethren spoke to the problem of divorce and remarriage. In part, it reads as follows:

Moses permitted divorce for trivial reasons but Jesus restored the original ordinance of God. Jesus permitted divorce for one reason — marital infidelity. A believer's union with Christ is more precious than an earthly marriage to an unbeliever. If the believer has to choose between the obligations of marriage with a non-Christian and the obligation to do the will of God, it is the latter obligation which must be recognized.

Jesus permitted remarriage for only one reason, marital infidelity. When married people separate for any other consideration than adultery the subsequent marriage of either party is a violation of the law of God. If anyone has left his companion for reasons of loyalty to God, they commit adultery if remarried and are excluded from church membership.

The statement of Menno Simons quoted earlier recognized adultery as the only ground for divorce and that a believer was not under bondage if deserted by an unbeliever.

Based on the statements of catechisms, a more rigid view was taken from 1690 to 1800. Fornication was considered just grounds for separation or even divorce but remarriage was not permissible for the "innocent" party.

From 1867 to 1900, a number of our district conferences faced the divorce and remarriage issue. In September 1867, the Virginia Mennonite Conference took the following action: "It was also decided that for the same reason that a man is allowed to put away his wife he is allowed to marry again." This was the same position set forth in the early Swiss Brethren tract.

In 1875, the Indiana Mennonite Conference took action to reinstate a brother who had married a divorced woman, and explained their decision as follows:

> The fact that he had been a brother, having known the requirement of the gospel as well as the rules of the church on this point makes it a very serious transgression, but if he truly repents and brings forth fruits meet for repentance, he can be received again according to 1 Corinthians 6:9-11. In reference to this matter it may be remarked that . . . the woman not being a member of the church, neither her first husband, they were out of Christ and hence under the civil law and being divorced under that law . . . she under the law was no longer bound to him, and we are taught that upon true repentance, all sin except blasphemy against the Holy Ghost shall be forgiven.

The Franconia Mennonite Conference decided in 1887 that a man married to a divorced woman could be received if the congregation voted unanimously in favor of doing so.

J. C. Wenger gives the following summary concerning the view of the Mennonite Church toward the turn of the century regarding marriage and divorce:

> It is thus evident that the prevailing view in the Mennonite Church in the latter decades of the nineteenth century was that marriage ought to be permanent. But where lives were broken

by sin, and people were divorced and remarried legally, and the Spirit of God then brought them to repentance and faith; our brotherhood then stretched out to them a welcoming hand and received them as members, in spite of the sins of the past. Our church then followed the principle, Whatever one's state was when he was called of God, let him abide in that state (1 Corinthians 7:17, 20, 24). [13]

However, after 1900, leaders such as Daniel Kauffman saw a second marriage relation, with the first companion still living, as a continuing sin. In 1905 Mennonite General Conference registered its belief that people holding a divorce "obtained for the sake of remarriage, or being married a second time, and continuing to live with the second companion while first companion is living, should not be received into the church." This remained the accepted position until around 1950 when a number of district conferences faced again the question of divorce and remarriage. Many adopted a position similar to that held seventy-five years earlier.

In summarizing the historic understanding of the Mennonite Church regarding marriage, divorce, and remarriage, we observe the following:

1. Marriage has always been viewed as instituted by God and for life. Believers are to marry only in the Lord.

2. Divorce has generally been allowed but only on the grounds of unfaithfulness.

3. During several periods in our history, some of the church understood the exception clause in Matthew 5 and 19 to mean that remarriage was permissible when the cause of divorce was adultery. These periods were (a) the beginning of the Anabaptist movement, (b) the latter decades of the nineteenth century, and (c) the present time.

A general summary of the current understanding of the Mennonite Church on these issues is difficult because of variation within the brotherhood. The following, however, can be noted:

1. Christian marriage is understood to involve man, woman, and God focusing on a commitment of faithfulness for life.

2. While unfaithfulness or adultery does not dissolve the marriage requiring separation or divorce, it does severely strain the marriage union and may cause separation or divorce.

3. When persons apply for membership who are remarried with their first partner still living, approval of the congregation is required before membership is extended. Some congregations would not grant membership privileges regardless of background circumstances while others would do so on a selective basis such as divorce due to adultery or divorce and remarriage prior to conversion.

4. The attitude of the church toward believers or members involved in divorce and remarriage is quite varied. In some congregations they lose their membership. In other congregations membership is retained. This urgent problem needs an answer today.

In light of the study thus far, the following position seems valid. If the marriage relationship deteriorates and the couple seems to be incompatible, or if a spouse is unfaithful, or if a couple becomes divorced emotionally, the Christian couple should by all means seek marriage counseling to again rebuild and rediscover relationship. Adultery does not automatically "break" the marriage because of the unconditional nature of their covenant. The Christian will not seek divorce when a partner has been unfaithful, partly because of the covenant, and partly because the assumption of an "innocent" and a "guilty" party is unrealistic. Both husband and wife must face their part in the state of emotional "divorce." The "innocent spouse" must honestly ask what part he or she played in causing the companion to be unfaithful.

However, if serious attempts to receive help through

counseling are unsuccessful and if staying together is injuring the physical or emotional health of the spouse or children (a physician's evaluation would be advisable), then the Christian may choose separation rather than staying together, or obtaining divorce. 1 Corinthians 7:10, 11. But separation must be seen as failure to keep their covenant and needs to be faced as sin needing forgiveness. The same is true of emotional divorce.

If the couple choose divorce rather than separation, they would be guilty of breaking their covenant. The relationship had already been broken; now the covenant would also be broken. In a sense every spouse fails to fully live his covenant daily and therefore needs the attitude of humility and forgiveness, but divorce brings a breaking of the covenant. Both separation and divorce are sins against the spouse and against God. (It should be remembered that even though divorce breaks covenant, the emotional and psychological union of personality developed through the total marriage experience will remain.) Will God forgive this sin? Yes, but forgiveness must be internalized to be personal and meaningful.

But what about remarriage? It would seem that a second marriage could then be formed in God's eyes. The individual would need careful preparation, giving attention to areas of need contributing to failure in the first marriage. He would need a personal sense of forgiveness toward his spouse and himself. He would marry only in the Lord. A second covenant would be entered into. A new relationship would be built. Sexual relations would not be an act of continual sin.

This conclusion attempts to hold a high view of marriage and at the same time deal redemptively with those whose marriages have failed and who have remarried. The church teaches that Christians shall marry only in the Lord, and yet it maintains a ministry to those whose spouses are not Christian. In the same way the church teaches the permanence of marriage but needs to provide a ministry to those whose marriage has not been permanent.

This chapter has attempted to set forth the biblical understanding of divorce and remarriage. The next two chapters will enlarge our understanding by examining divorce and remarriage from other perspectives.

CHAPTER 2

Why Do Marriages Fail?

Few would deny that the percentage of family failures is on the increase. The facts tell a tragic tale.

During the past two decades, one out of four marriages ended in divorce. Some authorities say one third of all marriages now end in divorce within ten years. Annually there are about 400,000 divorces in the United States alone. Some estimate that one half of all marriages are unhappy, and that only one in four appear to be stable and harmonious. In a recent research project, 80 percent of the couples interviewed said they had seriously considered divorce at one time.

The total number of divorced persons makes up a significant segment of society. The estimated 5.5 million divorced and separated men and women in the United States have their own subculture. According to *McCall's* magazine, 45 percent of the single, formerly married women in America are single by virtue of divorce — not widowhood or annulment.

While the facts of marriage failure are obvious, the causes are less obvious. Why do marriages fail?

Forces Destroying Marriages

It is difficult to identify all the cold winds blowing today that chill marriages. Some years ago, Professor Lewis M. Terman listed about sixty grievances spouses have about each other that cause serious trouble. M. R. C. Astley found four roots to marital tension: (1) immaturity of one or both partners; (2) character problems which involve distortions of personal values; (3) neuroses and psychoses with their attendant effects on the partner; and (4) situation reactions such as a business reverse or prolonged separation.

Narrowing the number of causes still further are Sylvanus and Evelyn Duvall who propose two basic causes of divorce. The first is a serious breakdown in character which cannot be corrected, such as the criminal husband who will not reform or the wife who continues to practice sexual promiscuity. The second cause is a basic incompatibility in which one spouse is going in an opposite direction from the other in terms of interests and values.[1]

A still more restricted view is expressed by F. A. Magoun, where he narrows the cause of divorce to incompatibility. "All else — cruelty, adultery, drunkenness," he says, "is merely rebellion against the frustration of incompatibility itself. Divorce is the result, not the cause, of failure."[2]

Whether the list numbers sixty or one, a careful examination reveals both internal and external causes. Internally, many people carry erroneous attitudes that weaken the foundation of marriage. Externally, certain factors in society are destructive in character and exert enormous pressure.

While it is true that what we feel from without and what we think from within are linked together and therefore difficult to examine separately, we can, for the purpose of our discussion, examine one facet at a time. We turn now to some of the sociocultural realities that profoundly affect family life.

External Social Patterns

Viewed sociologically, marriage in primitive society involved a relationship necessary for existence. "The family unit was a unit for physical survival."[3] Long, hard toil was the lot of every family member. The family with maturing children usually had added advantages, including greater chances for survival. Young children were a survival liability but older children played an important part in the survival activities of the family. According to some authorities "love" was not important.

It was during the Middle Ages that the word "love" as it is used today became current. The nobles in their castles became the leaders and protectors of the surrounding community. The lady of the castle held a position of prestige as did her husband, the lord. Being freed from the daily routine of work, the lady of the castle had leisure time to achieve a level of education that frequently rated above her husband.

But along with leisure came boredom and a preoccupation with her own appearance. When the nobles left home for war or travel, other men, including the troubadours, tried to amuse the ladies with songs and ballads about "romance." The result for many ladies of the castle was sexual looseness. Out of this social condition grew the concept of romantic love.

With the rise of female monarchs such as Queen Elizabeth and Queen Victoria in Great Britain, the phenomenon of romance grew even stronger. The courting period before marriage was characterized by romance, but after marriage the male frequently became a tyrant. Romantic love gave way to married love.

Immigrants from England brought the romance-before-marriage tradition to America. However, the romantic courtship pattern moved from the elite to become a common custom. The change was partly due to the shortage of women during pioneer days when men would compete for the few available females. The privilege of marriage went to the male most apt in romantic-love behavior.

A revolution occurred in the relationship between men and women during the periods of World War I and World War II. Women learned they could compete with men doing an equal or superior job in many activities. This began to bring an end to a male-dominated pattern in society. Women demanded equality in both society and the home. The home was no longer the primary place for women to find personal fulfillment and security. The marriage relationship was no longer a must for security and livelihood. The wife could go it alone if the marriage relationship was unsatisfactory. For many, divorce was viewed as an easy way out.

As men and women have become less dependent on each other, the character of society has fragmented and become depersonalized. The only setting in which people can act out their emotional needs and drives without restraint is in the home. This means that the greatest tensions and frustrations are expressed in the close relationship of marriage and it is here that it becomes most damaging.

People outside the home are in a competitive, critical, and often hostile environment where they have to act, to play a role, to conform, to pretend. In previous centuries a great many human contacts — with their emotional frictions and releases — were provided because of the larger families and the circle of relatives with whom contact was maintained, friendships, and participation in community life. The reduction of personal relations to an almost exclusive interaction with the marital partner puts an unbearable tax on marriage which few can endure over a long period.[4]

Economic factors have also brought new family pressures. Up to the nineteenth century, most people in the West lived on the land or operated family industries. The development of the steam engine by James Watt in 1769 started economic changes that led to changes in family life.

The rise of factories removed the husband from the home, thus placing upon the wife the burden of maintaining the home and caring for the family. As families moved into the cities, families often fragmented before the children were grown. Mothers were humiliated because they could not adequately care for the children and many fathers faced failure in providing for the family. Frequently the pressure became too great and Father would desert the family. Mothers then needed to work and soon sought further education to enable themselves to fill their new role more adequately.

A radical change was taking place in Western culture where the male had traditionally been dominant over the female. As the role of the man changed from reliance on physical strength to reliance on skill and intellect, the gap between the male and female roles narrowed. Women could now compete with men in economic life. Marriage was no longer entered into for economic survival but for an experience in partnership which often turned into a struggle for psychological and emotional survival.

While radical changes have taken place in the institution of marriage, sufficient adjustments have not developed to meet current demands. Individuals are unable to reconcile their traditional role image with current realities. The result is the battle of the sexes and family turmoil. The institution of marriage is in trouble. Marital strife, desertion, divorce, and emotional and physical illness are a few of the painful symptoms. Hopefully, out of the pain new patterns will emerge.

The religious history of marriage has also undergone considerable change. At its peak, the Holy Roman Empire used canonical law to exert control over all aspects of human life in Western Europe. Canonical laws regarding marriage were the most stringent. Prior to this time, marriage laws and customs had been civil, but then they came under the control of the church and marriage was made a holy sacrament.

The arrival of the Reformation and related developments removed much of the tight control of the Roman Church on many aspects of life, including marriage. Today marriage is viewed primarily as a legal contract. While the church is involved in many marriages, it is not involved in securing a divorce. Since divorce is primarily a legal matter, religious considerations are seldom taken into consideration.

Related to the change from religious to legal orientation for marriage is the changing attitude of the state toward divorce. In the past, some persons were discouraged from divorce by the demanding legal requirements. This is now changing. On January 1, 1970, a Family Law Act went into effect in California. The law is designed to smooth the path of the broken marriage. The new law does not "award" a divorce to the "innocent victim" of a "guilty" spouse. Instead, a marriage is dissolved if the court finds there are irreconcilable differences which have caused the "irremediable breakdown" of the marriage. The term divorce has been abolished. Instead there is a "dissolution" of the marriage. This is called a "no fault" law. Similar laws have been enacted in other states and the approach may well be the direction for the future. For better or worse, the number of divorces has risen in California since the new law was enacted. This would seem to say our nation and churches will face the issue of divorce in increasing frequency in the years ahead.

Internal Attitudes

In their book, *The Mirages of Marriage,* Lederer and Jackson discuss a number of false assumptions about marriage. These myths cause people to bring to marriage improper attitudes, assumptions, or expectations. When their assumptions are not fulfilled or their expectations not met, their commitment to the marriage is weakened. What are some of these internal attitudes or false assumptions?

First, there is the assumption that love is the primary reason for marriage. Romantic literature gives strong support to the idea that people marry because they are "in love."

Many couples discover after marriage that they are not as loving as they thought they would be. What has happened? Actually, unconscious drives such as loneliness, insecurity, self-improvement, sex, and approval are primary in taking many couples to the marriage altar. Few couples marry only because of love and few possess true love. The best definition of love appears in 1 Corinthians 13 but all couples must confess their failure to live this standard consistently. American Psychiatrist Harry Stack Sullivan says, "When the satisfaction or the security of another person becomes as significant to one as is one's own satisfaction or security, then the state of love exists."

I have frequently heard individuals with marital conflicts say that they no longer love their spouses. This is not surprising. Likely they did not possess the level of love defined by Paul or by Sullivan before marriage and the conflicts have made them aware of this deficiency. Not yet aware of the actual motivation for their marriage, they are ready to give up the venture for a true love which they will likely never find. Only if they discover the actual motivation for their marriage and the true nature of love, will they be able to begin building a solid marriage.

A second misleading attitude is that married people have a constant awareness of love for each other. Many have been preconditioned to assume that this is the normal experience in marriage. Research, however, indicates that most spouses who have been married more than three or four years rarely state spontaneously to an interviewer that they are in love. They more than likely speak of the husband being a good provider and the wife a good mother.

These qualities express a love relationship even though the spouses likely do not live with a constant awareness of mutual love. In fact, much behavior that is considered to be a loving act is actually a profoundly destructive act or an act that is basically selfish. The real test of a genuine marriage relation is not the amount of time spouses spend reflecting on their mutual love or the number of loving acts each feels he performs. Rather, it is the depth of genuine concern each spouse has for the well-being of the other.

A third false assumption, closely related to the second, is the mistaken idea that "love" is required for a mutually satisfying marriage. The evidence of both research and observation indicates that many husbands and wives are disappointed in their marriages. The high divorce rate, the constant flow of articles in magazines and newspapers dealing with female-male relations, and the crowded offices of marriage counselors all speak a loud message. Marriage seems to have a missing ingredient.

The illusive something called love for which so many couples long is more accurately described as romance. Romance is basically selfish in that it focuses on self-fulfillment. It blindly attributes to others qualities one wishes him to have because these qualities are desired for oneself. It assumes that the ideal marriage is an extended, ecstatic honeymoon. When a couple awakens from their "love" dream and discovers that married life is not "whirling around in a tornado of romance," they may feel the problem lies with the spouse and that they made the wrong choice. What they need is to discover that genuine love is best displayed by elderly couples whose functional union has the elements of "tolerance, respect, honesty, and the desire to stay together for mutual advantage."[5] In this relationship romance has given way to reality. A solid, accepting, and satisfying relationship has developed.

Fourth, there is the erroneous idea that having children automatically enriches an impoverished marriage. While children are an extremely significant factor in marriage, research indicates that many childless marriages are as successful as marriages blessed by offspring. Therefore, it cannot be said that children automatically help or hinder a marriage.

A marriage that is unhappy before the arrival of children may experience additional aggravation upon the arrival of children, due to the role they play in the relationship between husband and wife. A power struggle between the sexes can soon focus on the responsibilities and privileges each sees in relation to the children. This may take the form of wanting the exclusive affection of the child or of failing to accept responsibility for the care of the child thus putting additional burden on the spouse. While a child provides an opportunity for a couple to focus mutual love outside themselves thus enriching their relationship, this does not automatically happen. And if husband and wife have not learned to share responsibility before a child arrives, the child will not force sharing to develop.

A fifth illusion about marriage is that it will cure loneliness. When lonely people marry each other to overcome their loneliness, they usually discover that loneliness shared with another is a more painful and intense loneliness. There are several types of loneliness. The first type is experienced by persons with a limited behavioral repertoire. Their behavioral experiences have been so limited they have unusual difficulty interacting with other people. A second type, most frequent among males, is the person who unconsciously seeks triumph over others as a substitute for love. The individual may have lost his mother early in life thus having been deprived of love in childhood. He needs to triumph over others in some way in order to get along with them. The third type is usually seen in persons who had an intelligent, dominant mother and a passive father who acted as if he were inferior to her. Obsessed with the desire for approval and popularity, these persons have attractive personalities and social grace. But they have difficulty being intimate unless they are the center of attention. Persons described above are still lonely after marriage.

> Loneliness cannot be cured by marriage. Loneliness is better tolerated by those who live alone; they have no expectations, and thus no disappointments. Lonely people who live together have about the same chance of realizing their expectations as the host who insists that everybody have a good time at this party.[6]

Psychiatrist Clemens E. Benda has described another attitude many bring to marriage which ironically leads to the breakdown of many marriages. In the Western world, happiness and emotional satisfaction are considered fundamental to the mental health of the individual, the family, the children, and the community at large. If family relations are not satisfactory or if expectations of happiness are not achieved, the individual is faced with a difficult decision. Shall he continue a frustrating relationship with all its harmful personal effects, or shall he dissolve it recognizing there may be equally undesirable effects on all persons involved? This question would not be asked in many cultures as freely as it is asked in North America, where personal happiness is a primary goal.

A related consideration is that the focus of man's struggle has changed due to scientific conquest of the universe and industrialization. No longer is man's struggle focused on competing with a hostile nature striving for the fundamentals of living. The focus has now shifted to concentration on self-development and self-realization. Instead of looking outside himself in search of the means of survival, man is now looking inside himself in search of meaningful human relations.

Some authorities see such unsatisfactory relations springing primarily from omissions. If couples will put forth the effort to work out individual areas of competence and responsibility, arriving at a clear understanding of who is responsible for what, the way is prepared for a healthy marriage relation. Furthermore, if couples can see their differences as being differences rather than indications of inferiority, much of the potential difficulty will be removed. Couples should then approach marriage with the idealism that enables them to create the best possible relationship, but also with the realism which will enable them to settle for a marriage that is imperfect due to their humanity.

Requirements for Successful Marriage

Every person possesses a powerful heart longing to relate meaningfully with at least one other person. This longing may be conscious or unconscious in the form of a painful loneliness. Howard J. Clinebell, Jr., describes the inescapable need for human relationships as the "will to relate." He sees it as more fundamental than the "will to pleasure" discovered by Sigmund Freud, or the "will to power" described by Alfred Adler, or the "will to meaning" delineated by Viktor Frankl. The sum of these strivings — pleasure, power, and meaning — can only be realized in human relationships.

Our society exhibits many examples of "relationship-hunger." Loneliness and unhappiness are mild forms and personality distortions and mental illness are more severe forms. At the core of many marriage failures is lack of fulfillment of relational needs. Successful marriage can only be achieved when the parties involved are conscious of their basic need to relate and satisfy this hunger in the life of the spouse through growing intimacy.

As background for the book, *The Significant Americans,* John F. Cuber and Peggy B. Harroff conducted extensive interviews over a five-year period with 437 significant Americans. They discovered two basic types of marriages. Utilitarian marriages are established or maintained for some purpose other than a deep personal relationship between husband and wife. Personal considerations are not important and consequently there is limited companionship and the lack of empathic feeling.

Intrinsic marriages, on the other hand, put husband-wife relationships in first place. The primary concern is their common life together. They have obligations of career and family but they are somehow kept subordinate.

While Cuber and Harroff see many utilitarian marriages as being satisfactory to the persons involved, it is significant that many of the spouses find intimate relationships outside the family. In other words, if the universal "relationship-hunger" is not satisfied within the marriage relation where God intends it to be met, other relationships will be developed in an attempt to satisfy this felt need. A basic requirement, then, for successful marriage is a satisfying, fulfilling relationship.

Examining the marriage relationship more closely, we discover five patterns of husband-wife relations as described by Cuber and Harroff.[7]

The conflict-habituated relationship contains an amazing contradiction. For these couples fighting is a way of life. However, the strong tension and conflict are controlled. They fight verbally, not physically. Out of a basic need to do battle, they experience a kind of intimacy. Relationship is experienced through the exchange of hostility.

Second, there is the pattern of *the devitalized relationship*. For these couples, the blossom of love in early marriage has faded. The fires in their marriage relation have gone out. They think of themselves as having been "deeply in love" in past years, but now little time is spent together and few interests are shared. Some are resigned to their condition expressing the opinion that this is normal for couples in the middle and later years. Others are deeply dissatisfied and long for the good old days, but they seem unable to revive their earlier pattern. In both cases their point of intimacy is being partners in a relationship that has almost died.

The passive-congenial relationship is the third pattern. It resembles the devitalized relationship with the exception that it has always been passive. Life is lived on the level of a low-key sameness. These couples cannot look back to a brighter yesterday because their relationship has always been this way. Some couples develop this pattern through design. Their primary interests are outside their own relationship and they have not attempted to create a deep level of intimacy. Other couples have drifted into this pattern by default. They have not cared about each other deeply enough to share life in its fullness. Regardless of how their pattern of relating developed, they are not troubled by memories of the past when life together was more fulfilling.

The fourth pattern of marriage is *the vital relationship*. In an average day, these couples do and say many of the same things as types one, two, and three but there is added a high degree of intimacy. They feel bound together psychologically. The presence of the spouse is necessary for activities to be fully satisfying. Most of these couples know their style of life is different from the average but they enjoy the difference. These couples have conflicts but they come only from major issues, not trivial matters. Disagreements are settled quickly so as to avoid conflict and maintain intimacy.

The fifth and final pattern is *total relationship*. It resembles pattern four but has in addition numerous points of vital meshing. A level of vital sharing is experienced in all important areas of life. There are few areas of tension because past differences have been resolved as they arose. In resolving conflict, their important concern is not who is right or who is wrong; rather, their concern is to resolve the difference without hurting the relationship. Obviously this pattern is the highest level of intimacy.

As these patterns of marriage have been examined, it has become evident that marriages are evaluated on the basis of their degree of intimacy. This would seem to be the proper criteria because as Gibson Winter has said, "Marriage is intended to be an intimate relationship. This is the one opportunity for sharing one's whole life with another person."[8]

Since the degree of intimacy is the criterion for evaluating a marriage, it is necessary to consider how growth in intimacy is achieved. Many couples realize a shallowness about their marriage relationships and would like to have them deepened, but they seem unable to initiate growth in intimacy. Clinebell lists four basic requirements for the deepening of the marriage relationship.

First, a couple must risk greater openness. When a spouse risks personal honesty in facing his own faults and stops blaming the other partner for their conflicts, the wall that separates them begins to crumble. When spouses see themselves as fallible persons, they can accept their own shortcomings and those of others. A spirit of tolerance can then emerge. To close off emotionally charged subjects putting them off grounds for discussion begins to build a wall or blur the relationship. "Intimacy thus requires mutual openness and the willingness to risk genuine encounter or meeting in areas which are important to either partner."[9]

Second, a couple must learn to be emotionally present to each other if they are to grow in intimacy. To be truly present speaks of an at-homeness where feelings, ambitions, fears, and thoughts become links between husband and wife. A spouse can easily be in the same room with the partner yet feel in a different world.

Third, couples will grow in intimacy as they develop a high degree of caring for each other. Where there is genuine interest in the partner's growth, well-being, and work, there will be growth in the relationship. True caring is demanding, involving continued self-giving. But it becomes mutually satisfying, for caring involves both giving and receiving. It involves being warm and open to the needs of each other.

Fourth, couples will grow in intimacy in a climate of trust based on commitment to fidelity and continuity. If marriage is viewed as an experiment in living together, little intimacy will develop. Or if a spouse finds his basic needs being met outside the marriage, the chances of intimacy are slim. To grow in intimacy, a couple must recognize that "we're in this thing together" and not give up in times of conflict or crisis. Then and then alone will true intimacy develop.

This discussion of requirements for successful marriage has focused entirely on the various facets of the marriage relationship. This approach implies that the nature of the husband-wife relationship is the most important single factor in marriage and that a sharing relationship is absolutely essential for fulfillment in marriage. Is this approach valid? Yes, because as Clinebell has well said, "troubled marriages are essentially hungry marriages."[10] Basic heart-hungers are not being fed. Fundamental emotional needs are not being met. When basic heart-hungers are met through an authentic, intimate relationship, emotional needs are satisfied. What are these needs?

First and foremost is the need to love and be loved. The human heart yearns for someone to love. To live alone cut off from the opportunity of knowing and loving another person is to stop living emotionally. This is one side of the love coin. The other side is to be loved. Leslie B. Salter says: "Every normal man or woman longs more keenly for love, for warm friendship, admiration, and human responsiveness from his fellows than for anything else in life. . . ."

To experience love is to know that another person cares about me in a deep, accepting way. This is an indispensable need of every person. It is to this basic need that all other needs relate. The human ear longs to hear another say, "I love you," and the human heart longs to feel another express in verbal or nonverbal terms, "I care."

> The kind of love which is the glory and wonder of a marriage — growing love — represents an integration of all the facets of intimacy which the couple has cultivated in their relationship. The integration of sexual, emotional, and spiritual intimacy, for example, makes each of these facets of intimacy richer and more soul-satisfying. Tenderness and passion, comfort and confrontation, dependency and autonomy — all are woven into the multicolored fabric of the emerging "we-ness" of marriage.[11]

A second basic need is communication in depth. In marriage there is constantly an attempt to bridge the gap between the solitariness of me and solitariness of you. When one party in a couple refuses to bridge this gap, then communication is impossible. The result is frustration and bitterness.

To speak of being estranged means that two persons who have been intimate have again become strangers. Long before actual divorce takes place, the couple is likely involved in "emotional divorce." They have ceased communicating on a depth level and are talking on surface issues. Or even worse, their communicating is in the form of destructive quarrels rather than problem-solving discussion. A magazine cartoon pictured a husband and wife leaving the office of a marriage counselor. The husband was saying to the wife, "Now that we've learned to communicate, shut up!"

Security is a third basic human need. Security has been described as an "inner feeling of stability and safety that comes to a person in a relationship in which he feels a sense of identity, acceptance, belonging, and being wanted."[12]

This inner feeling can only develop if there is evidence of

genuine fidelity in the marriage relationship. There must also be a constant sense of acceptance even when a spouse realizes the partner is falling below his hopes. This acceptance recognizes that a mate has certain defenses and vulnerabilities that are related to him being a unique person. These are respected and not attacked when the going is rough. When husband and wife stand by each other in the difficult and distressing circumstances of life, then the need for security is satisfied.

In summary, it can be clearly affirmed that man's social and emotional hungers are only fully fed through intimate interpersonal relationships. Marriages are successful to the degree to which they meet these needs.

In the discussion of requirements for successful marriage, attention has not been given to the spiritual hunger of man and the way in which this hunger also needs to be met for total wholeness of life. Failure to discuss this area is not meant to indicate its lack of importance. Rather, I see the spiritual dimension of husband and wife as one of the large and significant areas of life that can be shared only when both spouses are experiencing a vital religious faith. The concern of the Christian counselor is that both spouses possess authentic faith so that this area of life can also be intimately shared.

In this chapter we have examined both the external and the internal forces contributing to the breakdown of marriage. It is important for the counselor to be aware of these forces because couples are often not aware of the reasons behind their disintegrating relationships. If the counselor can help a husband and wife gain this insight, the partners are in a better position to take constructive steps to improve their marriage.

An examination of requirements for successful marriage has shown the primary importance of intimate relations, how to deepen them, and why they are so significant for total wholeness of life. It is important that the counselor have this insight because the only hope for a crumbling marriage is to build a better relationship. Only then will a couple be able to move from alienation to intimacy.

CHAPTER 3

Is Divorce the Answer?

At the Bella Vista Motel, the man in Room 27, is having a bad night of it: his light has been on and off half a dozen times since midnight. Room 27 is comfortable enough: the motel is hardly four years old, everything is still new and attractive, the bed is firm, the air conditioner is working properly. But the buttons in the mattress annoy him, the air conditioner seems noisy, the lights of passing cars make patterns through the Venetian blinds. He gets up and turns off the cold air, but in ten minutes is sweltering; he turns it on again and soon is chilled. He pulls up the blanket, sighs, and begins to drift off, only to wake with a start, thinking, Is it really true? Can this be happening to me? Sweat breaks out all over him; he goes to the bathroom for water and a tranquilizer, sees himself in the mirror and winces: the fleshy face looking back at him, usually strong and ruddy, is ashen, dough-soft, and red-eyed. What am I to do now? he wonders. He will be forty years old in two weeks: too early to give up, too late to start again. He scowls at himself and utters a curse, disgusted at his own rather ridiculous self-pity.

Rather ridiculous, because he is facing neither imprisonment, ruin, nor major surgery. What happened to him this evening happens to three thousand Americans every day of the year: he and his wife have just broken up and are headed for divorce. [1]

Morton M. Hunt begins his informative book, *The World of the Formerly Married,* with this graphic and tragic incident. Literally the incident did not happen but figuratively it has happened thousands of times.

Is divorce the answer? Does this ridiculous tragedy of human experience bring the desired results? Is the road from Reno the road to happiness?

The Emotional Cost of Divorce

The emotional cost of divorce is usually extremely high. Often individuals only think of the release of getting out of their unhappy marriage. They do not consider feelings with which they will have to live.

William J. Goode speaks of these feelings as "divorce trauma." On the basis of extensive research, Goode concludes that the time of final separation is the point of greatest disturbance, not immediately following the final decree. "The impact or disturbance rises from (a) the point of final decision to (b) a high point at a final separation, then (c) tapers off very gradually to the point of first filing, and (d) drops somewhat further to the point of the final decree."[2]

The observation placing the highest trauma at the time of final separation agrees with the incident described by Hunt. He characterized the time of greatest stress as the point when the couple has just broken up and are headed for divorce.

Research indicates that the trauma index varies greatly depending on events leading up to divorce and the type of separation experienced by the couple. However, for most couples, the road through divorce is a long and painful process that includes a number of emotional reactions.

There is the loss of self-esteem. A husband invests considerable time, money, and effort in building a home. If this disappears, a part of him is gone. A wife's feelings of success to a large extent focus on her success as a wife and a mother. If she fails in this area, her failure looms very large. Both spouses then lose esteem in their own eyes and in the eyes of many of their friends. Some friendships will be permanently lost.

Where custody of the children is involved, there will be difficulties with relatives on both sides. The grandparents may not understand the limitations on visiting the children. When the divorce is contested, the divorce process becomes a clan fight. Feelings become even more hurt as the legal divorce takes place.

The loneliness and drastic change in personal habits become very significant. Both parties may have to find jobs. New friendships need to be cultivated. Plans for retirement likely evaporate. Arrangements for the children's education may be drastically changed. The road is always covered with emotional bumps and chuckholes.

Nancy Love, writing in *Philadelphia Magazine,* describes graphically the various sides of the divorce experience. In "Everything You Always Wanted to Know About Divorce (But Were Afraid to Ask)," she reports interviews with a significant number of divorced persons. The tone of the article is expressed in these few words: "For most divorced or about-to-be divorced people there are ups and downs: bouts of loneliness and rejuvenation, dislocation and increased productivity, isolation and sexual rediscovery, awakening and despair — especially at first.[3]

Having looked at the general "divorce trauma" and emotional disturbance related to the divorce experience, we turn now to specific emotional reactions attending the experience.

Guilt from an awareness of failure is foremost among the painful feelings. There is guilt over the broken marriage itself. Whether spoken or unspoken the person feels he was unable to succeed. Generally divorcees examine their behavior before the divorce and feel guilty about many of the things they did. Also, they accuse themselves of things they might have done. Often the failures on which they focus are not the crucial items in the breakdown of the marriage, but they cause deep guilt nevertheless. "The divorcee usually blames himself for causing the behavior in his mate which led to the conflicts which finally brought about the dissolution of the marriage."[4]

In addition there is often guilt over events that took place before the marriage, such as a premarital affair or hostility toward a parent. Actually these unresolved guilts may have contributed to the divorce.

Another disturbing emotion is grief. In the deepest sense, divorce means death. A person with whom there has been a close relationship is now permanently gone. A part of him has died. "The mood at divorce is seldom elation — by either party — it is usually numbness, anxiety, and a sense of being in a fog. These are the same problems that come at death."[5] The divorcee often goes through a grief process similar to a spouse who has lost his companion in death.

Goode sees the nature of the grief experience related to divorce as being different from grief related to death. The separation brought by death has a unique sense of finality different from separation by divorce. Furthermore, the separation by divorce is the climax to a long period of conflict that has reduced the emotional attachment between husband and wife. This would suggest a lower level of grief.

James H. Burns feels that both the divorcee and the grieving person have lost an "emotionally significant person." However, the divorcee has helped to bring about the loss by working for the divorce. This factor may cause feelings of both grief and guilt. Another consideration is the fact that death confronts a spouse with an irreversible reality, while with divorce the former spouse is still in existence and may even live in the same community.

Hostility is a third emotion experienced by the divorcee. The emotional turmoil experienced by many divorcees reduces their ability to relate meaningfully with those they do love. This leads to further isolation and expresses itself in annoyance and hostility toward friends and relatives who are trying to maintain the close relationship they had before the divorce. After experiencing hostility several times, the friends are ready to stop trying to be friendly. They are frustrated in their effort at friendship. And the divorcee cannot understand his own feelings and is sure he is "going crazy."

Many divorcees find that feelings of anger, hate, and hostility well up in great bursts usually stimulated by kindness from a friend. These feelings impress divorced persons as being different from any previous bad temper for which they might have had a reputation. They have a sensation that their feelings of rage may overwhelm them or, in some inexplicable way, lead them to a senseless act of violence.[6]

Another emotional reaction of the divorcee relates to his identity. Some describe this as an "oddball" experience. The newly divorced person is in a strange category. He is not married, neither is he single. He goes through a new identity crisis as he attempts to discover who he is.

Being unsure of his identity, the newly divorced person often becomes dependent on any person who will extend friendship. But this relationship may itself become strained by open resentment expressed in such terms as accusations of attempting to run his life. The divorced person's inner conflict with his identity causes outer conflicts.

Finally, certain physical symptoms are commonly experienced by the divorcee. Many find that their five senses seem to play strange tricks on them during the early months of divorce. Abnormal taste and smell sensations often alter eating patterns. If the food has no taste, some do not eat regularly and lose weight. Others stuff themselves with food in an absentminded way. Many complain of changes in their vision. While looking at a friend, they have the feel of staring through a hollow tube. Frequently they appear to be inattentive or hard of hearing. Some complain of feeling neither heat nor cold. Sensing such changes in patterns, they assume they are approaching a nervous breakdown.

> Most divorcees experience, during these months, attacks of easily recognized physical symptoms which usually last fifteen minutes or more. The attacks are characterized by dryness in the mouth and throat, difficulty in breathing, a mild nauseous feeling in the stomach, generalized weakness, and an all-pervasive sense of mental and physical misery.[7]

Children also suffer emotionally when divorce destroys the family. From 150,000 to 200,000 children in the United States each year become "children of divorce." Authorities vary in their evaluation of the emotional effect divorce has on children. Some maintain that the divorce experience is always damaging to the children and therefore should be avoided at all costs where children are involved. Others feel the scars of constant home conflict are harder on children than divorce. There is evidence for both points of view, but all recognize that divorce is traumatic for children.

A major factor affecting children is the frequent absence of the father. Both boys and girls need a father figure as an object of love and security. (Special emphasis is placed on the absent father because he is the parent most likely away from the family.) When the parent is absent because of divorce rather than death, children experience unique feelings of hostility, guilt, and abandonment. It is impossible for one parent to fill the total vacuum created by the absence of the spouse.

Parents considering divorce and having a concern for their children need to evaluate their situation. A fundamental question is whether the negative effects of the divorce are greater than those of constant conflict in the home. Of course, ideally they should be putting forth every effort to improve the present home situation.

If divorce does come, both parents should make every effort to reduce the emotional hurt of the children. Studies show a direct relationship between the level of divorce trauma of the mother and the change in the behavior of the children. Specific suggestions for parents securing a divorce will be considered in Chapter 2 of Part II.

The Futility of Divorce

Is divorce futile or fruitful? To discuss the futility of divorce may sound like an unobjective approach to the question. Perhaps it is because evidence is available to support both its futility and its fruitfulness. An example of the fruitful attitude is the statement of a mother of four children who stopped therapy after two or three sessions. She divorced and remarried. About five years later, she defended her actions to John F. Cuber and Peggy B. Harroff.

> I had become a psychological mess and I knew it — so did my husband, and so did my friends. The kids didn't miss it either. So I left him. . . . It's a lot quicker, less costly, and less disorganizing than going to the couch. I know. I tried that too. All I got from it was a feeling of resignation and apathy, which I almost went for. . . . But I couldn't really learn to live with the nothingness. . . . What I needed was the right man. . . . Now everybody says I'm so different — my health, my appearance, my outlook, my work — everything!

William J. Goode believes we have not done sufficient research to answer accurately the question of whether second marriages are as happy as first marriages. However, he observes that "those who do divorce a second time seem to have a shorter second marriage than first marriage. . . ."[8] Furthermore, he finds that three times as many divorcing partners had divorced parents as had parents who stayed together.

Edmund Bergler in his book, *Divorce Won't Help*, holds that neurosis is the cause of much divorce. If the neurotic elements which destroyed the first marriage are not adequately corrected, the second marriage will likely experience similar difficulties.

Following the insights of Freud, Bergler describes neurosis as "the child in you, though to all external appearances you are a grown-up person. If you have a neurosis it means that you have retained in your unconscious infantile conflicts — desires, defenses, feelings of guilt — which under normal conditions you would have overcome between the ages of one and five."[9]

Bergler sees neuroses as silent partners in neurotic marriages. Each spouse has an "invisible unconscious partner," who is actually the deepest part of the real person, yet the spouse is unaware of his presence. He is like a little fox who spoils the marital vines.

In an unhappy marriage the neurotic person projects his own inner conflicts on the spouse. The neurotic person assumes that divorce will end the unhappy chapter of his life. He assumes that a change of external factors will change his inner conflicts. By sending away the person on whom he has projected his conflicts, he believes he will be driving his conflicts out of his home and life.

The neurotic's futile attempt to escape conflict is described in the following quotation.

> A neurotic conflict is unconsciously dramatized in marriage. The stage is set, and the partner is chosen in accordance with the rules governing the specific neurosis. The partner is unconsciously viewed not as a real person, but merely as a movie screen upon which to reel off an unconscious conflict. Divorce means that unconsciously the person suing for divorce wants to get rid of her own inner conflict. Unaware of the very existence of the conflict, she fights with great energy against her partner, upon whom the conflict has been projected. In other words, she has confused her unconscious dynamic conflict with her husband, and thus the internal battle is not fought on the real front. The displacement is usually mutual; hence the spectacle of two people who want to get rid of each other.[10]

The obvious solution to a neurotic marriage is healing the neurosis through the help of a counselor, not dissolving the marriage by an attorney. Bergler rightly concludes that, for neurotic marriages, divorce won't help. But what about marriages that experience conflict where neurosis is not the cause? Is divorce futile for them?

Not all sick marriages can be healed with professional help. Many factors, such as the motivation and capacity of the spouses, contribute to the possibility of saving a marriage. No person can be forced to change his pattern of interpersonal relations or life-style. But most sick marriages can be greatly improved when both spouses have the honest desire to work at it.

Sylvanus and Evelyn Duvall see a certain amount of marital conflict as normal for most couples. Husband-wife relations have their low points just as most people occasionally become sick or injured. If couples would seek help from qualified counselors when their marriages become sick, just as they secure help from doctors when their bodies become ill, most critical problems could be avoided. Friends, relatives, or strangers may help bring relief from minor pain but not from major illness. To rely on these concerned persons rather than a doctor may prove fatal. The same principle applies when marriages become ill. "Many marriages that finally end in divorce were first painfully ill or damaged. But, with understanding care, many of them could have recovered as sound, healthy marriages. In many cases, the marriage didn't die. It was killed through bungling or misinformation."[11]

Many families with "major illness" have been healed through the services of family courts or similar agencies. The legal profession in general considers reconciliation desirable between estranged couples. The courts are increasingly providing opportunities for marriage counseling. In New York, Rhode Island, Lucas County, Ohio, and Los

Angeles, family courts have been set up. Family courts are concerned not only with saving marriages but also with humanizing the proceedings. Court-appointed counselors interview husbands and wives in an attempt to help them work out differences or agree on the arrangements for settlement.

The court in Lucas County, Ohio, mandates counseling for every case. Sometimes they advise a cooling-off period before proceeding further. This provides time for the partners to consider the many involvements of proceeding with a divorce. Said one husband after searching through the questions, "Before I sink great quantities of my time, energies, emotions, and money into breaking up my home I'm going to see if a similar investment, made now, can help to keep it together. . . . Divorce is hard work; while I still have a chance, I'd rather work hard at living with a marriage."

The Los Angeles conciliation service offers optional counseling and the possibility of working through a written agreement of understanding. Over 60 percent of the persons referred to the California Conciliation Court have remained together with some 75 percent of these remaining together after one year.

Cook County, Illinois, also has a Conciliation Counseling Service. In their first year of operation they counseled 572 families. Two hundred and forty-three families involving 632 children were reconciled.

The high rate of success experienced by these counseling agencies supports the position that, in most cases, divorce is not necessary. Healing and reconciliation are within reach.

I recognize that it takes the cooperation of both spouses to build a mutually satisfying marriage. There are times when one spouse refuses professional counseling and may insist on divorce. In such situations there may be no choice but to grant dissolving the marriage. However, there have been many situations where only one spouse was deeply concerned about their shaky marriage. The unconcerned spouse occasionally spoke about divorce but was not taking aggressive steps. Through the initiative of the concerned spouse in securing counsel and in being a positive influence in the home, family relations were greatly improved and a potential divorce averted. Whenever the "will to succeed" exists, the likelihood of divorce is greatly reduced.

Is divorce advisable? In answering this question consideration must be given to the emotional cost of divorce. Guilt, grief, hostility, identity crisis, and psychosomatic symptoms — all these feelings accompany the divorce experience. The counselor needs to help persons considering divorce become aware of the price they will pay. Furthermore, the involvement of children and the effect on them must also be taken into consideration.

The counselor should help persons considering divorce face the futility of such action. If the cause of conflict is a neurotic condition, divorce will not resolve the inner conflict. If professional counsel has not been secured, this needed help should be sought just as a person with physical illness goes to a doctor. As long as there is life there is hope. Where some degree of life exists, the counselor will encourage taking steps to renew life rather than choosing death.

Part II
COUNSELING PROCEDURES

CHAPTER 1

A Model for Pastoral Counseling

In Part I, we focused on Counseling Perspectives. The concern was to become knowledgeable in those important background areas which relate to divorce and remarriage. Attention was given to the biblical teachings, the factors that are causing widespread divorce, and the nature of the divorce experience. The pastor-counselor needs these perspectives to help guide his own understanding of divorce and to bring an objective perspective to the person considering divorce or remarriage.

In Part II we now shift our focus to Counseling Procedures. The central concern deals with methodology. How does the pastor go about counseling persons considering divorce or remarriage? We will first explore basic principles in counseling and then apply these principles to the concrete situation of counseling persons considering divorce and persons considering remarriage.

First we will review historic developments in counseling to help us understand the significance of a contemporary model. The basic approach to counseling has changed during recent years and we can only understand the significant point of progress in light of the past. While the model presented may not be acceptable to all pastors, it does represent the primary pattern in pastoral counseling today and represents a partial movement toward the older authoritarian approach. The model corresponds with the pattern I have found to be most effective and personally most acceptable.

Pastoral counseling has been a major concern during

the centuries of the Judeo-Christian era. Albert L. Meiburg has traced the rich and varied heritage of the pastoral counselor. His discussion appears in Chapter 1 in *An Introduction to Pastoral Counseling* edited by Wayne E. Oates. A brief summary of this heritage follows.

The concept of counsel or counselor was central in Jewish life and thought. Two Hebrew words, *sodh* and *etsah*, meaning couch and counsel appear over 100 times in the Old Testament. The Jewish understanding of the Messiah's role was of one who would give counsel (Isaiah 9:6; 11:2). Jesus of Nazareth fulfilled this expectation as we observe in Luke 4:18 and John 2:25.

The Epistles of Paul indicate he engaged in pastoral counseling involving quarrels between Christians, interfaith marriages, divorce, illicit sexual activity, and relations between master and servant, husband and wife, and parent and child. Several of the church fathers saw the importance of the counseling role of the pastor. Chrysostom's *Treatise on the Priesthood* is one of the classical treatments of pastoral care. Ambrose of Milan wrote *Three Books on the Duties of the Clergy*.

Pastoral care during the medieval period was given secondary attention because of the church's preoccupation with theological controversy. We do know, however, that the parish priest was the most educated person in the community and that "men turned to him as lawyer, doctor, teacher, counselor, and friend. The sacrament of penance was a basic influence in this period and involved contrition, confession, and satisfaction." [1]

The Reformation brought a fresh emphasis on pastoral counseling. Luther himself gave considerable attention to counseling concerns in his sermons, commentaries, and letters. His *Letters of Spiritual Counsel* reveal his pastoral heart. Martin Bucer attempted to develop the church into a community of love where Christians would receive individual guidance. His book, *On the True Care of Souls,* describes his concern. For the Reformers the confessional was dropped as a sacrament and in its place emerged the pastor-counselor and priesthood of all believers.

During the nineteenth century, outstanding changes developed in pastoral counseling due to the influence of Horace Bushnell and Washington Gladden. Bushnell stressed the importance of the early years in personality development. Gladden understood the close relation between physical health and mental health. He observed that there are some things "the doctor with his drugs can never cure, but that would be quickly put to flight if the load of shame and remorse that are resting upon the heart could be removed." These developments laid the foundation for a scientific approach to pastoral counseling.

Jonathan Edwards pioneered in the psychology of religion by writing his outstanding work, *A Treatise Concerning the Religious Affections.* Other major writings in the same field soon appeared. In time, pastoral counseling was enriched by the mature development of the psychology of religion and later the development of clinical pastoral training.

Anton T. Boisen, the father of clinical pastoral training, had a most significant influence on pastoral counseling through his clinical training program. Hiltner, Wise, and May studied under him and later wrote significant books related to pastoral counseling.

Developments in psychology have caused the approach to pastoral counseling to undergo major changes. Frederick C. Kuether, writing in *Pastoral Psychology,* characterized these changes by a series of questions. The counselor's original concern, he says, is "What must I do to be of help to the person?" The question then changes to "What must I know?" then to "What must I say?" and finally to "What must I be to be of real help to the person?" Obviously the

75

emphasis had shifted from doing to being.

The primary approach to pastoral counseling during the past decades has had an effective spokesman in the person of Carl R. Rogers. His influential books include *Client-Centered Therapy, Counseling and Psychotherapy,* and *On Becoming a Person.* Terms used to describe this approach are "client-centered" and "psychoanalytic." Rogers' influence is so widespread that Clinebell writes about the pre-Rogerian period, the Rogerian period, and the emerging post-Rogerian period.

The Rogerian approach is basically insight-oriented with an emphasis on uncovering psychotherapy. The pastor-counselor assumes a relatively passive stance in an attempt to help the client receive self-understanding. It is assumed that changes in feelings and self-perception bring about behavioral changes. If a person feels right, he will act right. If he has a proper self-image, he will perform properly. Seward Hiltner well expressed this point of view when he wrote:

> The generic aim of counseling is new insight, with proof in action. That is, if a person is troubled about his situation or some aspect of it and seeks a helper through counseling, the end which all such professional helpers have in common is to aid the person to get a sufficiently clear view of his situation, with the conflicting trends and pulls and motives and ideals and desires, that he may then see his situation in a freer, clearer, more objective way and consequently be able to act in a similar new fashion.[2]

Clinebell lists the following five basic concepts that gave direction to pastoral counseling during the nineteen forties and fifties:

(1) The formal, structured counseling interview as the operational model;

(2) the client-centered method as the normative and often exclusive methodology;
(3) insight as the central goal of counseling;
(4) the concepts of unconscious motivation, and
(5) the childhood roots of adult behavior.[3]

Even though insight-oriented counseling sounded like the ideal approach, the results were not always ideal. Reflecting on his experience in counseling, Clinebell says that "this approach is useful with reasonably intelligent, verbal, young or middle-aged neurotics who are strongly motivated to get help."[4]

The practical problem faced by many pastors is that a large number of persons who come to them do not have the ability to respond to a passive approach. The counselor and client experience the mutual frustration of endless hours of talking but no substantial change occurs in patterns of living. These persons are not capable of achieving the necessary insight perhaps because they lack ego strength or because their personalities are too rigid.

Pastors generally need the discipline of the Rogerian approach to teach them the real art of listening and the importance of responding to feelings. The older approach for the pastor was being the problem solver or advice giver. Playing God in the lives of the parishioners was often the result. Rogerian technique came as a needed corrective. But the pendulum seems to have swung too far in the other direction. Today the call is for a revised model.

The new model as projected by Clinebell is person-centered instead of client-centered. Rather than primarily seeing himself as a detached counselor, the pastor brings himself to the situation. The new model is "relationship-centered" in that the pastor views his relationship with the counselee as an important part of the counseling. Instead of creating "distance" between himself and the counselee, the pastor is free to reveal his own humanity. He attempts to create a healthy relationship with the person being counseled recognizing that many of the counselee's problems are related to his unsatisfactory interpersonal relationships. Experiencing healthy relationships is important for the personal growth of the counselee. The pastor recognizes his rightful authority and, when necessary, uses it to guide, teach, encourage, or confront.

Another aspect of the new model is its emphasis on conscious rather than subconscious material. Most pastors are not equipped to uncover unconscious motivations or analyze childhood experiences. And if they are knowledgeable in these areas, the limitations of time make depth counseling impossible. The new model recognizes that most counseling done by the pastor is of short-term nature and by focusing on current problems and immediate future plans, significant growth will be experienced. It recognizes that a relationship must be established with the counselee as a person, not some remote "it" which needs to be analyzed. The pastor views himself basically as a shepherd, not a psychotherapist.

In *Pastoral Care in Historical Perspective*, Clebsch and Jaekle list four historic functions of pastoral care:

(1) Healing — a pastoral function that aims to overcome some impairment by restoring the person to wholeness and by leading him to advance beyond his previous condition.

(2) Sustaining — helping a hurting person to endure and to transcend a circumstance in which restoration to his former condition or recuperation from his malady is either impossible or so remote as to seem improbable.

(3) Guiding — assisting perplexed persons to make confident choices between alternative courses of thought and action, when such choices are viewed as affecting the present and future state of the soul.

(4) Reconciling — seeks to reestablish broken relationships between man and fellow man and between man and God.[5]

These four historic functions are uniquely necessary in today's counseling. The Rogerian approach emphasized healing through gaining insight and gave guidance a secondary role. Sustaining and reconciling were likewise given secondary attention. The new model emerging today recognizes all four areas of need as being of primary concern for the pastor. Furthermore, healthy relationships are significant in bringing aid in all four areas of need.

Frequent reference has been made to a new model for pastoral counseling. The principle of the new model and its contrast with the Rogerian approach has been examined. The five basic concepts of the Rogerian method were noted. The uniqueness of the new model becomes even more evident when we examine its basic concepts.

(1) using supportive rather than uncovering methods;

(2) improving relationships (through couple, family, and group methods) rather than aiming at intrapsychic changes;

(3) maximizing and utilizing one's positive personality resources in addition to reducing negative factors;

(4) coping successfully with one's current situation and planning for the future rather than exploring the past extensively;

(5) confronting the realities of one's situation, including the need to become more responsible, in addition to understanding feelings and attitudes;

(6) making direct efforts to increase the constructiveness and creativity of behavior as well as feelings and attitudes;

(7) dealing directly with the crucially important vertical dimension (the dimension of values and ultimate meanings) in relationships as well as the horizontal dimension of physical and psychological interaction.[6]

Earlier it was noted that the new model is much more usable by the average pastor since the primary focus is on the present rather than the past. The major concern deals with interpersonal relations rather than psychotherapy.

Another important factor should be noted. Not only is the new model more usable, it is also uniquely suited to marriage counseling. This is true in several respects.

First, the focus is on improving relations through the persons with whom the counselee relates closely. Marriage problems obviously involve problems growing out of relationships in the marriage. The troubled relationships may be with one's spouse, children, parents, or relatives. By dealing with relationship changes rather than intrapsychic changes, the focus is on the actual point of conflict in such a way as to involve those who share in the conflict. This is taking the most direct route to the problem under consideration. Furthermore, when focusing on relationships, the pastor is dealing with the single most important aspect of marriage as was noted in Chapter 2. Any amount of psychological insight will not help a crumbling marriage unless there is a resulting change in the relationship between the spouses.

A second major concern is facing one's situation realistically including the need to become more responsible. This concern touches the root of many marital problems. A lack of personal responsibility is a primary factor in many strained marriages. The failure may spring from general immaturity where the spouses are quite young or it may relate to one or both spouses failing to function in the expected roles and manner. Facing a failure in personal responsibility stops the guilty spouse from placing the blame on the partner.

Third, this approach deals with values and ultimate meanings. A Scripture frequently applied to marriage is, "Can two walk together, except they be agreed?" This implies the need for couples to share similar values and goals. Surface conflicts between spouses frequently reflect deeper conflicts between goals. Counseling that is effective needs to probe this vital aspect of the marriage relation.

Having noticed the distinctive features of the new model for pastoral counseling we turn now to the basic elements of the counseling process. Short-term pastoral counseling usually involves from one to five interviews. In listing the basic elements of counseling, I am indebted to Wayne E. Oates and Howard J. Clinebell, Jr.

First, the counselor should listen carefully and respond to feelings. A person with problems serious enough to request an appointment will generally talk freely during the first interview. He "should be left completely free for any emotional outpouring of immediate apprehension and of his own confused impressions of the cause of this condition. In case of weeping, intense agitation, and acute anxiety, he should be allowed to pour out his feelings, and no attempt should be made by the counselor to control or stop such expression."[7]

The emotional catharsis experienced by the counselee in verbalizing his problem is essential. Response to deep feelings through facial expressions or similar means will communicate acceptance and in turn encourage freedom to share. Oates indicates that the counselor "should give himself to that person's story with complete abandon. This abandon and dedication enables the person to talk more easily and clearly."[8] In the first interview, at least one half of the time should be given to concentrated listening.

If the counselee is not conscious of time and engrossed in unloading his problem, the pastor may have difficulty beginning a discussion of the problem areas. An effective approach might be to say, "I understand the extreme difficulty you have been facing and your feeling that something specific must be done." Such an approach assures the counselee of your feeling with him and suggests it is now time to turn the attention toward finding help.

Second, the counselor should raise questions essential to providing necessary information. Some important details were likely omitted from the "story." Relevant questions are beneficial to both pastor and counselee. Directing questions carefully so as to focus on areas of conflict or strongest emotions enables the counseling session to move rapidly to the most important concern.

It is also helpful to discover whether the person came for counsel out of his own desire or whether he decided to respond to the pressures of some other person. If pressures of spouse or parents brought the counselee to the pastor, little positive good can likely be accomplished. The pastor will need to indicate his desire to help but the counselee must desire to be helped if progress is to be made.

Another question is whether the person has sought help from other counselors. If so, when did this take place and over how long a period of time? Some individuals are seeking an ear for sympathy but are not willing to face realistically their contribution to the problem or conflict.

After the pastor has clarified the problem in his own understanding, a third step is to "play back" the total problem as the counselor sees it. This step gives the counselee the confidence that the pastor has grasped what he is struggling with and often helps to clarify the real situation for the counselee. I have observed individuals receive a more objective view of their situation as a result of this step. Sometimes they wonder why they were so upset. The problem no longer looks as big as it did before.

Fourth, explore the alternatives. What are the viable choices open to the individual and what are the likely consequences of each one? Wayne E. Oates has observed that "people under pressure tend to be able to see only one alternative for solving a personal problem. Yet, one of the reasons they come to a counselor is that they are not sure of this alternative. Therefore, one of the most important things a pastor can do is to search with the counselee for additional avenues of release."[9] In the words of one person, before counseling, she had "muddled around in the problem" without thinking about her options and their implications.

Guidance is the fifth step. Having arrived at the desired alternative, some assistance may be needed in how to proceed. Seeing the progression of events to bring about desired ends is important for beginning progress. Persons with major problems may have become immobilized by the weight of worry and thus find even a small step of action difficult. The pastor must be sensitive to this possibility and give guidance as needed.

Finally, there is need for spiritual support and inspiration. The fact that the counselee came with a problem indicates that it is too heavy for him to carry alone. Every counselor has discovered the reality of the statement, "Walk softly, for every man you meet is carrying a cross." The counselee needs a friend to walk with him and help carry the load. Since pastor and people together make up a fellowship of suffering pilgrims, spiritual support should be a normal climax to a counseling session. "The careful use of religious instruments — prayer, Scripture, sacraments — can deepen and enrich brief counseling by reestablishing contact with resources beyond the human relationship. The pastoral counselor confronts, but he also comforts! He challenges, but he also cares. It is the bringing together of these two paradoxical dimensions (judgment and grace) which produces growth in counseling."[10]

The primary focus of this study is on marriage counseling. Therefore, we need to move from basic elements in counseling to marriage counseling in particular. However, before looking at the final phase of this chapter brief attention should be given to some of the marriage distress signals. The alert pastor knows the values of anticipating problems before they develop. The marriage counselor knows the importance of danger signs because they may open the door for preventive counseling. Paul E. Johnson lists a number of early warning signals.

Absentmindedness usually suggests preoccupation. The

concept of a Freudian slip has become well known in our society and is looked upon with varying degrees of seriousness. Most would agree, however, that anxieties and worries are expressed in absentmindedness and preoccupation.

Aggressive joking can be a subtle form of attack on another person. A sharp joke in a social setting may be considered "safe," whereas the same jibe at home would prove explosive. Behind such activity is evident hostility and a conflicting relationship.

Apathy and fatigue express a basic dissatisfaction or boredom. "When a marriage partner is indifferent to good times and shows no initiative in planning things the couple may do together, it may indicate a letdown in the desire and responsibility to keep love growing."[11]

Compulsive activity reflects a desire to escape some anxiety, insecurity, discomfort, or guilt. These persons have an obsession to keep busy but they seldom achieve success or reach real goals. While this pattern may not have developed due to marriage it can place a strain on the marriage relationship.

Frequently, sharp clashes which develop are symptoms of a sick relationship. In addition they tend to cause suppression of touchy areas that are "off limits" for conversation. As these areas grow, the common ground for conversation shrinks, placing additional strain on the marriage. A third party is often needed to open conversation and enable each spouse to share honestly his feelings so that mutual understanding and respect can develop.

Loss of common interests is an evidence of declining love. This development is usually gradual as each spouse becomes absorbed in separate interests. Outwardly they attempt to appear intimate but inwardly their lives have become distant. They are only together when necessity demands and find greatest satisfaction when each goes his own way.

The pastor carries a special concern for healthy marriages. He performs many wedding ceremonies and learns to know the couples in premarital counseling. His desire is to see each couple growing in a satisfying marriage relation. When these distress signals are observed, he may choose to give help indirectly through teaching and preaching or he may feel the situation warrants a direct approach. If the pastor takes the initiative or if the couples take the initiative in coming to the pastor, what should the pastor-counselor attempt to do?

Clinebell describes marriage counseling as role-relationship counseling. The totally unique aspect of every marriage is the way the couple relates. The nature of their interaction determines the nature of their marriage relationship. A couple needs counseling when their marriage relationship becomes "sick." When this happens, the relationship is the "patient." The major goal in marriage counseling is to enable the relationship to become mutually need-satisfying. How is this accomplished?

We have examined the basic elements of counseling. These elements become the structure in which counseling takes place. We need yet to look at the specific goals the counselor works toward as aspects of the major goal. Clinebell defines these goals as follows:

(1) Reopen their lines of communication.
(2) Interrupt the vicious cycle of mutual retaliation.
(3) Face the need to work together in strengthening the relationship.
(4) Become aware of the nature of their interaction, particularly the ways in which it produces pain in both parties, and the roots of their interaction in their role images.
(5) Learn how to learn from their conflict.
(6) Have experiences of thinking together about sources of pain and pleasure in their marriage, followed by planning and working together toward mutually set goals.

(7) Face the futility of their campaigns of mutual reformation, and begin to "release" each other, and accept the unchangeable aspects of their relationship.

(8) Begin to do something about their own areas of irresponsibility in the marriage.

(9) Begin to discover and experiment with new ways of relating which produce more mutual satisfaction of personality and sexual needs. Experience the satisfaction cycles of more mature relating.

(10) Find a focus of concern outside the family and a more satisfying relationship with the "extended family."[12]

The first three goals are followed in sequence. The others have no special order and may be met as the relationship improves.

In this chapter, we have traced the historic development of pastoral counseling giving special attention to the rise of the client-centered approach. The new model with its stress on the relationship-centered approach received major attention since this is the approach that will be followed in the next two chapters. With the concept of the new model in focus, we viewed both the basic elements of counseling in general and the goals of marriage counseling in particular. These insights will be applied to specific counseling situations in subsequent chapters.

CHAPTER 2

Counseling Persons Considering Divorce

The preceding chapter dealt with the theory of counseling. We turn now to an application of the theory as it relates to counseling persons considering divorce. We will begin by examining a verbatim account of an actual counseling situation. The case study selected is typical of the type of case a pastor frequently faces. The approach of the pastor will be evaluated in light of the model developed in the preceding chapter.

Then we will focus on how a pastor can assess a troubled marriage. This step is necessary before guidance can be given. A second basic step we will explore is the examination of options. This step is necessary in attempting to help a couple reach their own decision.

Finally, we will consider the role of the pastor during and following divorce. It is assumed that even the best pastor-counselor is unable to heal certain sick marriages and these couples may choose divorce. Therefore, the pastor must be prepared to go through the experience with the couple. Attention will be given to the nature and scope of his role.

Case Study

The following case is taken from *Casebook in Pastoral Counseling* edited by Cryer and Vayhinger.

I received a frantic call from a stranger one evening asking if "we can come and see you right away." I had never heard of the couple before, although the caller told me they had lived in town about six months. I told him I would be glad to see him. It made me late for an official board meeting, but it was worth it. When the couple came in, I could see there was difficulty between them. The husband, Jack, started in.

Jack: I wanted to come up and tell you the story first, but she insisted on being here, too. Betty, now you keep still for five minutes until I've told him how it is, then you can talk all you want to.

(I said nothing. She slumped in the chair and was still.)

Jack: Betty and I have been married two years and eight months. I was married before for ten years and had four children.

Betty: Only three — the last one wasn't yours, and you admit it.

Jack: Yes, but that's all past. The trouble is, Betty thinks I should just ignore and forget my kids by this other marriage. I agreed to give their mother $120 a month for their keep, and now when I want to send a Christmas gift Betty blows up and the fight is on.

(He said he was making good money — $675 a month — as dispatcher on the railroad, but it meant being away from home three days a week. While he is gone she gets silly ideas that he still loves the other woman because the former wife sends "mushy" letters which Betty insists on opening and reading, including between the lines.)

Betty: We still owe the doctor for the first of the two babies, and we owe everyone in town — he won't let me see what he's sending — more to those kids than he says; because look at me, I have had two maternity dresses since we've been married. I haven't any stockings. I can't go anywhere because he gives me only two dollars a week — sometimes not even that. All I want to do is go home. I don't want to live with him anymore — he beats me. When I was eight months pregnant, he beat me. (She pulled up her coat sleeve to show marks on her arm from the beating.)

Jack: I didn't hurt you, and you had it coming.

Betty: If you mean I didn't lose my baby, no; but it did hurt, and if you were half a man you'd know it.

Jack: Well, when she gets to harping on a thing for days on end, I just can't take it anymore. So I clipped her. It was the only way to shut her up.

Pastor: Uh-huh. (She began to cry in great wracking sobs. I turned to him.) Was there any liquor in this?

Jack: No, I'm not a drinking man — couldn't keep my job if I were. Neither of us drink. It's just her incessant nagging, and I guess I've got a temper.

Betty: (She had quieted enough to tell me that during the summer the oldest boy by the other marriage had been with them.) My baby (a year-and-a-half old) didn't have any shoes, but when Mike comes, even though he has two pairs, Jack takes him up-town and buys him another pair. There isn't any money to buy us clothes, but that kid has three pair of shoes. All I want is to go home. (Fifteen hundred miles away. She has no relatives or old-time friends here. Just a few neighbors.)

Pastor: Well, the best cure for homesickness is to go home.

Jack: Homesickness, bah.

Pastor: Is it homesickness or are you trying to run away from a problem?

Betty: All I know is I don't love him anymore. I just want to leave him.

Pastor: (I turned to him again.) There are three things on which a home can break up — finances, sex, and lack of religion. So far I've learned one of these. How about the other two?

Jack: Well, she's a Methodist and I'm Christian Scientist; but I haven't been to church for years.

Betty: You're a no-good Mormon.

Jack: I was raised a Mormon, but I quit that long ago.

Betty: And as for sex, he certainly doesn't consider me at all. He couldn't wait two weeks after the baby was born.

(He was very embarrassed and tried to think of some way to change the subject. I waited.)

Betty: I'm a Methodist, that's why we came to you.

Jack: We couldn't go on this way; we've got to have help.

Pastor: Would you like to have a third person help you work out a budget that would enable you to meet your obligations?

Jack and Betty: Yes.

Pastor: Could I come to your home tomorrow and help you?

Jack: That will be fine. We do appreciate your help.

Betty: Do you think I should go home?

Pastor: That is for you to decide: if you can afford it, if this is the right thing to do; and if it won't appear to others and yourself that you are running away. Can you get transportation, since you are on the railroad?

Jack: Sure, I've told her I could get her a ticket and she can ride a pass part way, but I don't like her running away. (She seemed just frustrated at that point, with a "trapped" feeling, if I read the expression on her face correctly. Obviously she was desperately unhappy; but she was a pretty woman, and despite the oldness of her clothes still had pride in appearance.)

Pastor: One of the things which helps the most to hold families together is prayer. I wish you were in our fellowship here.

Jack: I can't come because of my work.

Betty: You don't know how to pray anyway. Doesn't the church have a good Bible study book of some sort? (I handed her a copy of *The Upper Room*, commenting that it could help in family prayer. I also gave her E. Stanley Jones' *The Way to Power and Poise*. Before they left she had *The Upper Room* creased tightly in the middle and rolled up.)

Pastor: It appears to me that there are several things we can do to help. I'll be glad to come and help work out a budget with you; and if you stick by it, it will help your financial problem. So far as the letters from the other woman are concerned, Betty, will you promise to ignore them? If you can't resist them while they are around the house, just put them back in the mailbox and they may not get back to you until Jack is home. Could you do that?

Betty: That's bad. (I wondered if I sensed a martyr complex in Betty's attitude at that point.)

Pastor: And Jack, will you try to curb your temper? There is a Christian proverb that he who first resorts to physical violence admits he has lost the argument.

Jack: Sure, I'll try, if she'll just quit her nagging. (They both grinned.)

Pastor: Let's not leave out a single resource that can help. Would you like a word of prayer? (They agreed.)

Pastor: God our Father, help us to keep our faith in Thee and in one another. Help us to know Thou art ever in the shadows keeping watch above Thine own. Help Jack and Betty to find the way to peace in their hearts. Amen. (Then I asked them to join me in praying the Lord's Prayer. They both knew it and prayed it. She was in tears again as we finished.)

Pastor: Jack, you have a beautiful wife. (The smile that came through her tears was beautiful.)

Jack: I know it, and I want to keep her. (As they went down the steps he held her arm.)

SECOND CALL

A phone call the next morning from Jack indicated he felt I needn't come. Betty was going home. I urged him to let me come and see them anyway.

Jack: Sure, you're welcome to come, but it won't do any good. When a woman gets her mind set on something, brother, that's it!

Pastor: I would like to come, and unless you definitely do not want me to, I will be there about three o'clock.

Jack: Okay, we'll see you.

(When I arrived Betty met me at the door with a very gracious smile. Jack came in from the kitchen and was affable but tense toward her. Perhaps there had been some acrimonious exchanges before I came.)

Pastor: Jack said on the phone that you have decided to go to Los Angeles. Does that mean you intend to make it permanent? (She merely nodded. Tears were close again.)

Pastor: Are you sure you want that, Betty?

Betty: He doesn't love me anymore, and it will be better all around.

Jack: You know that isn't so. I do love her, but she has her head set on going, so I guess that's all there is to it. I've asked for a pass for her.

Pastor: That doesn't mean it must be used, does it?

Jack: Oh, no, but they don't like it if you bother them for a pass and don't use it.

Pastor: For the sake of this youngster (a seventeen-month-old boy came toddling in), I hope you can find some way to maintain a home. I'd like to help on that.

(The floodgates of acrimony were released again, as on the night before. He invited me into their closets so I could see that she did have lots of clothes and he had very few. My comment was that women seem to need more. He admitted none were new. The old wounds were gouged and probed with devilish glee, until I broke into the exchange.)

Pastor: I wonder if you are doing any good by rehashing all these hurts that are in the past. We all make mistakes, and dwelling on them makes both ourselves and others miserable. I believe the important thing is seeing that.

Jack: Here we are. Where do we go from here?

Pastor: One road is separation, but there are other ways. One other is to forget the past and push forward together. Do you want to explore that?

Betty: Yes. (He was noncommittal.)

Pastor: Do you still want help on a budget, as we talked about last night?

Jack: Our problems aren't financial. We can work that out if she would just get over her jealousy. She nags about my former wife and she gripes about my going to a show when I'm in ————; but with forty-eight hours between shifts I can't just sit in a hotel room; I've got to do something, and what else is there than a show?

Betty: Would you like a sheet of paper so we can work out a budget?

Pastor: Yes. (She got it arranged on a kitchen table and brought a big envelope which evidently contained back bills. We listed all the expenses they had; and after including something for medical expenses, for clothing, for amusement, and for church and charity, they still had forty dollars which could go on back bills. She seemed amazed that there could be something left.)

Betty: Why haven't we done this together before?

Jack: Because you don't have any sense of money, either. Just like my former wife. (Aside to me.) You'd see something you wanted, and if you could write a check you'd get it and "blooie," there goes the budget. Or else you'd get mad at me about something and blow it all just to spite me.

Pastor: You need to do things together, whether it's going to a show, to church, or just figuring out where the money is going. Why don't you come to the family-night program next Friday at church? Bring something for the meal. (They agreed to do that.)

Pastor: May I make one more suggestion? It appears to me that the problem of us all is inner control. For example, when we are faced with a budget like this, we stay within it; or when something irritates us, we don't throw salt shakers or whatever is handy; or when someone says something to hurt us, we just bite our lips or tongue instead of answering. It's not easy, but it is the only real control we have, and it's worth the effort. But I've preached enough to you. I do hope you'll come Friday.

Betty: Yes, I think I know right now what I'll fix.

(My departure was again on a level of good rapport, but how truly they want to work out their problems I don't know. I hope I keep the contact.)

PASTOR'S COMMENTS

I am wondering if I preached to them too much and if I was too insistent on seeing them the second time. It seems to me a place where aggressive action was needed, but I have qualms about such tactics. I have made four calls in the home since the last interview recorded here. The home has been saved and they are getting along all right. She comes to church, but his work still prevents his coming.[1]

An evaluation of the pastor's approach to counseling as compared with the model described earlier reveals both strengths and weaknesses. The pastor failed to respond to feelings during the first part of the first interview. He did play the role of a listener at first but too quickly began asking poorly timed questions and reaching ungrounded conclusions. The questions raised early in the interview were not essential for securing necessary information. Furthermore, the pastor failed to play back to them what he heard them saying, and how he heard them describing their situation.

The concept of several alternatives was mentioned but only one was explored. He did not offer to explore the possibilities of separation and divorce. The pastor did take strong initiative in giving guidance and attempted to give spiritual support. His comments at the close of the interview indicate he felt he had been too aggressive but that the marriage had been saved. A more accurate comment might be that aggressive action had prevented an immediate separation but that a sick marriage had not yet been fully healed.

A second approach in evaluating the interview is to examine it in terms of the specific goals in marriage counseling as described in the preceding chapter. Were the lines of communication reopened? Hardly. There was communication between both spouses and the pastor but the spouses were still arguing between themselves rather than truly communicating on important issues.

The pastor did make a definite effort to interrupt the vicious cycle of mutual retaliation. In this area he had some success. When he says that the home has been saved and they are getting along all right, he really seems to be saying they have stopped their fighting, not that they have solved their basic problems.

It appears some progress was made in the couple facing the need to work together to strengthen the relationship although this seems to be only a beginning.

The seven goals which follow these first three seem distant for the couple. Realities such as facing irresponsibilities and learning how to learn from conflict seem quite remote to their experience. It is a bit early to say the marriage is saved.

In concluding this phase of the evaluation, several observations should be mentioned. First, this couple is an excellent example of the type that would not respond to a passive, nondirective approach in counseling. The pastor needed to be aggressive to make any progress.

Second, the pastor's persistence in helping them make a budget may be questioned. Was this the most important activity at this stage of the counseling procedure? Not likely.

Third, the approach of seeing both spouses at the same time during the first interview was not the best method. If he had talked with each spouse alone and then both together, both would have been free to tell their story without interruption from the other. Both could have heard the pastor reflect his understanding of their basic conflicts.

Fourth, the pastor's insistence on going to the couple's house for the second call may not have been wise. The professional approach to counseling rules out "going after" people. If they will not take the initiative to come to the counselor, little good is likely to result. However, the pastor knows there are times when he must "go after" people if there is to be any opportunity of giving help. Apparently this was one of those situations, because the wife would likely have gone to her home if the visit had not been made at their home.

Assess the Marriage

The model for marriage counseling developed in the preceding chapter sees the counselor carrying a rather aggressive role. The aggression is not in terms of authoritarian pressure but in terms of actively working with the couple to help them resolve their basic conflicts. To fill this role, the pastor must assess a sick marriage just as a doctor must diagnose an illness. Questions to be considered are What are the basic conflicts? and How serious are they?

Many disturbed couples do not understand the source of their difficulty. The pastor in the case study was partly correct when he listed finances, sex, and religion as three common reasons for the breakup of homes. Actually these factors are more likely areas where deep resentments find expression. The pastor's main concern is to discover the actual, deep resentments.

One approach in attempting to make this discovery is for the counselor to draw out from each spouse his feelings about why he married in the first place. Was it to meet a personal need such as security or status? The counselee may not be able to express the real reasons clearly but the answers will give the counselor a deeper "feel" of the marriage. The pastor will be listening primarily for expressions of deep resentment or frustration.

John Charles Wynn provides a helpful suggestion when he says:

Many pastors use some mechanical device such as a checklist to guide their search for background and undercurrents of the marital rift. Among the customary topics that evoke some response are attitudes toward money, in-laws, premarital experiences, vocation, fears, guilt, religious faith, quarrels and making up, parenthood and children, health conditions, childhood memories, home conditions, and avocations. Each counselor tends to concentrate on his own set of most useful topics. Always, however, he is listening for that feeling tone that reveals basic attitudes and degrees of self-acceptance. If the person cannot stand himself because of guilt, inferiority, or some neurosis, he will be unable to accept his spouse, family, job — or counselor. [2]

Reflecting again on the case study, the pastor saw finances as the basic problem and immediately drew up a budget. It appears that the actual cause of deep resentment had not yet surfaced and the pastor was not determined to seek out the deeper problem.

When the basic conflicts do emerge, the pastor must make some judgment of their severity. In Chapter 2, we discovered many different causes for divorce. Sylvanus and Evelyn Duvall listed the two basic causes as a serious breakdown in character and a basic incompatibility. From their point of view, these two conditions represent an impossible situation and therefore justify divorce. In my opinion, these conditions represent an extremely difficult situation for both the couple and the pastor but the decision to end the marriage must not be made by the pastor. He continues working with the couple, knowing it is possible for God to do the seeming impossible.

It has been estimated that 50 percent of the present happy marriages would have terminated at an earlier period if divorce had been easily available.

The counselor does not look at conflict and resentment as being abnormal. They can be a normal part of any close relationship. His task is to discover as accurately as possible the basic problem or root of resentment so he can focus attention on the "target" area.

When the pastor has discovered the basic conflicts and

evaluated their seriousness, his next step is to assess the stage of deterioration in the marriage. Is the marriage "entering the rapids" or is it just ready to "flow over the falls" and be dashed to pieces? In other words, is the marriage sick or is it critically ill? Does the pastor have time to work with the couple at their speed or does he need to take aggressive steps in an attempt to rescue a perishing marriage?

Wayne Oates discusses eight stages of conflict in his book, *Protestant Pastoral Counseling*. Samuel Southard has summarized them in outline form in *An Introduction to Pastoral Counseling*.

A. Typical Adjustmental Conflicts
    1. Conflict over fear of pregnancy vs wife's working
    2. Living conflict over definition of adequate routine; i.e., agreeing upon a schedule — work, prayer, eating, sleeping, sexual relations, social engagements
    3. Conflict over communication failure
    4. Conflict over in-laws, especially financial, housing, and vocational involvements
    5. Conflict over spheres of dependence and independence, masculine and feminine role definitions
    6. Conflicts arising out of transferred or dated emotions
    7. Revelation of a defective covenant

B. The Stage of Serious Conflict
    1. Assaults upon each other's integrity
    2. Appearance of deception and withdrawal of the real selves; subterfuge
    3. Stalemate of communication

C. The Stage of Private Misunderstanding
    1. Agreement upon their helplessness; total resignation at attempts to communicate
    2. Individual isolation, loneliness, and anxiety of communication
    3. Search for an understanding person
    4. Alcohol, drugs, excessive spending, etc., as solaces; sexual deviations; pickup type of sexual escapades

D. The Stage of Social Involvement
1. Going to members of parental families for understanding; in-law involvement
2. Going to a third person of the opposite sex; extramarital activity
3. Development of community gossip
4. Going to a formal counselor

E. Threats of or Attempts at Separation
1. Threats to leave
2. Socially acceptable separations: changing jobs for travel opportunities, going home for summer; entering military service, etc.
3. "Going home to mother"
4. "Kicking" one another out, especially for drinking

F. Legal Phase
1. Going to a lawyer for advice as to rights
2. Private discussions of division of property, custody of children, etc.
3. Institution of divorce procedures
4. Conflict over grounds for divorce or giving one another a divorce
5. Social pressure from outsiders on either side

G. Divorce
1. Conflict over alimony, etc.
2. Conflict over seeing children

H. Postdivorce Bereavement
1. Shock: "not me" feelings
2. Numbing; loss of interest in other things
3. Struggle between completely breaking and trying to reconcile the relationship; legal break not final; the question of remarriage
4. Flood of grief, characterized by much hostility and repressed need to admire; sexual deprivation; economic insecurity
5. The grief-work period: selective memory, reassociation, one working through of feelings; loneliness; popular expectations of divorcees

6. The recharting of affections and discovery of new relationships; encounter of biblical dimensions of divorce; emotional readoption of children to meet needs left unmet by husband or wife
7. Remarriage [3]

Examining the case study in light of these eight stages of conflict, we observe that the couple in the interview was only one step from the lawyer. The wife was ready to go home to mother. If the pastor actually assessed the marriage as being at this critical stage, and apparently he did, he had good reason to be aggressive, even to the point of going to the home.

Examine the Options

Stage E, according to Oates, is the time for making basic decisions regarding whether a marriage shall continue. Some authorities believe that when a couple on the verge of divorce comes to a counselor, they are really saying they see only one option but are not completely satisfied with that option. The pastor's task is to explore with them additional options.

Behind this task is the assumption that the couple must ultimately make their own decision. David R. Mace has expressed well the dilemma a pastor faces when dealing with the possibility of divorce.

He is not simply a professional person doing a professional job. He is a representative of the church — of his own particular denomination, and of the wide Christian community that has been active in the life of the world for nearly two thousand years. He wishes to be loyal to the historical Christian tradition. He wishes also to serve his day and generation. It is not easy to reconcile these two wishes. [4]

In spite of how the pastor feels about divorce, some couples will decide to take this course of action. The pastor must allow the couple to make their decision. Clinebell suggests that being involved as a participant does not mean the counselor makes difficult decisions for the counsel-ee. If a person asks, "Should I get a divorce?" the counselor should recognize his desire for authoritative advice but make it clear that this is a complex decision that only he can make. No one else can make it for him. But the counselor will help him think through the various options and the possible outcome of each.

If the pastor is fortunate enough to be in conversation with the distressed couple before they have decided on divorce, he has the advantage of being able to work with them before the pressure of the crisis clouds their minds. The research of Cuber and Harroff revealed that "when divorce occurred. . . , it typically came as an 'end of the rope' decision after a period of three or four or even as long as ten or twelve years of awareness — usually mutual — that the marriage was unsatisfactory." [5]

Preventive counseling, which is done by many pastors, provides the opportunity for the early detection of marital conflicts. When serious difficulties are detected before the crisis stage, the pastor has a wide choice of helpful programs to offer the couple. These options can be discussed with the couple and they can decide which approach they wish to follow.

One option is to follow the "fix-it-yourself" method. The couple agrees to devote time to the serious study of books on marriage written by competent authorities. The pastor may need to suggest specific resources. *The Intimate Marriage* by Clinebell and Clinebell is an excellent one.

A second option for a couple is to counsel with a competent, neutral adviser such as a pastor or a doctor. A concerned pastor will offer his time and interest but will not be offended if the couple should choose some other counselor. Not all pastors are gifted or trained as counselors.

Third, most cities have a Family Service Bureau that provides professional aid to families in distress. Many local agencies are affiliated with the national Family Service Association of America. Usually a charge is made based on the counselee's ability to pay and the counselors are competent social workers. These agencies are used by people from all levels of society.

Fourth, most large cities have qualified marriage counselors. To be qualified requires years of special training and an advanced degree. Persons should not take the personal risk of going to an unqualified counselor even though he advertises in the telephone directory.

A psychiatrist should be consulted if serious emotional disturbances are evident. Most psychiatrists are not trained to deal with the ordinary difficulties of married life.

Some large cities offer a sixth possibility, a marriage counseling clinic. Philadelphia, Los Angeles, Detroit, and Topeka offer this type of counseling facility.

Finally, some areas of the United States have an organization known as Divorcees Anonymous. Their approach is that divorce is not a solution to marital problems. Like Alcoholics Anonymous, they offer twelve steps to recovery. Their meetings offer mutual therapy through group counseling by persons who have experienced the grief of divorce. Active members subscribe to five basic attitudes that comprise a type of creed.

1. Divorce is not a solution.
2. Marriage is a holy and desirable estate.
3. Development of future generations of physically, mentally, and emotionally sound persons depends upon the health and soundness of marriage and the family.
4. There is a spiritual power greater than man whose help is essential.
5. A willingness is needed to help others to a deeper understanding of, and better adjustment to, the married life. [6]

Obviously, most pastors cannot offer all seven options discussed above for securing needed counsel. Communities vary greatly in the types of counseling services available. But each pastor should become knowledgeable concerning the counseling services of his community. Only then can he present them to needy persons as counseling options.

The more difficult task for the pastor is discussing options when a couple is in Stage E of Oates' stages of conflict. Frequently they come to a pastor discussing their decision to divorce. What options can the pastor discuss in this crisis situation?

The first basic option is to enter seriously into a vigorous counseling program. We have just examined seven types of counseling services and most of them are effective if the couple really wants help. However, the first question concerns their willingness to cooperate in a program of counseling. This option is frequently acceptable if they have not had previous counseling. Most couples see the absurdity of filing for divorce without having made a serious attempt at resolving their conflicts through the aid of an able counselor. Of course this option, as is true of all options, requires the willing cooperation of the couple. When only one spouse agrees to seeing a counselor, some help will be received but it will be limited. Frequently the spouse who refused counseling at first will consent later if he senses a positive change in his companion.

When the pastor discusses the option of counseling, he should give some idea concerning the nature of the counseling procedure and the length of time required for maximum benefit. Without this understanding the couple may give up counseling before there is sufficient time for a fair trial period.

Another item of consideration, when discussing this option, is a reminder of the covenant made to each other and God at the time of marriage. The covenant was made recognizing there would be conflicts in marriage but that each would be faithful to the other even in the midst of conflicts. The fact of covenant should not be used as a pressure tactic but as an appeal to conscience. Ultimately the couple must decide.

A second option that does not require legal action is trial separation. As the term implies, the couple tries separation for a period of time. It may be by mutual consent or by the insistence of one spouse. Frequently the wife goes home to mother. This gives the couple an opportunity to test their love and find out if they still care for each other. If this option is chosen, the pastor should maintain contact with both spouses because both will need his objective guidance and support.

If the couple refuses the option of counseling or trial separation and insists on dissolving the marriage, some legal steps will likely be necessary. Under no circumstances should a pastor give legal counsel lest he open himself to charges by one or both spouses. He should, however, be acquainted with the state laws regarding separation and divorce.

Legal separation provides a third option. Goode sees separation as being more burdensome than divorce.

> In divorce, the relationship between the ex-spouses is at least spelled out in part by the decree itself. The parties are free to find substitutes for each other. They may be able to find emotional security or at least solace with other people. The situation has become officially defined, even though there are major gaps in the institutional definitions. The legal rights and obligations are definite, if minimum. In separation this is not usually the case, and it may characteristically serve as a temporary measure to alleviate severe conflicts. The assumption of their group may be that, after a while, they may possibly live together again as man and wife. [7]

I would confirm, on the basis of my own observations,

the validity of Goode's attitude. I have seen the conflict that can develop between separated spouses due to a lack of clarity regarding their relationship as legally separated spouses. But I have also seen legally separated spouses decide to live together again as man and wife. The pastor should be aware of these possibilities and refer to them when the option of legal separation is discussed. The likelihood of separation having some unclear areas should not rule it out as an option.

If the couple professes to be Christian and accepts the Bible as the guide for life and conduct, they will take seriously the teachings of 1 Corinthians 7:10, 11. When a couple cannot continue living together, says Paul, they should separate and then either remain unmarried or be reconciled. Chapter 1 of Part I discusses this position. The act of legal separation does represent failure to live up to the marriage covenant but it does respect the covenant and leave open the possibility of reconciliation. The husband partially fulfills this responsibility by providing maintenance and support for his wife and children.

Annulment is a fourth option for some marriages. In brief, annulment is the legal process whereby it is declared that a marriage has not been properly constituted (as when a bigamist conceals the first marriage and "marries" another partner). Legal counsel would be required to determine whether there are sufficient grounds to build an acceptable case. Generally if a marriage was established by force or one or both members are below legal age, the marriage can be annulled.

The fifth option is divorce. Divorce is the legal process whereby a marriage is actually dissolved. Criminal action applies to charges of assault and battery, neglect, desertion, or contributing to the delinquency of a minor. Civil action applies to petitions to dissolve the marriage, actions for support and alimony, and for custody and right of visitation and/or companionship with the children.

When a Christian couple is considering divorce, the pastor should help them face the biblical teachings as they were discussed in Chapter 1 of Part I. Christ's teachings should not be held over the heads of the couple as a religious club but neither should they be ignored. Christian spouses should honestly face the sin of divorce.

All couples considering divorce should face the emotional cost and the futility of divorce as discussed in Chapter 3 of Part I. Divorce is never an easy escape from a difficult situation. Many persons are affected, not only the spouses. The pastor in the case study was rightly concerned about the baby boy and his need to have a solid home. These areas should be discussed with the couple so that they can make their decision on the basis of all available information.

Each of the five options or alternatives should be explored, where applicable, and the probable implications examined. The couple should attempt to project ahead one or more years and see themselves living with the consequences of each option. Is that what they really desire? Would they deliberately choose such a future? No person can totally decide his future but life today is largely the result of yesterday's choices. In similar fashion tomorrow's life will largely be determined by today's choices. This principle should be understood by the couple as they make a major decision.

Pastoral Care During and Following Divorce

Pastors usually experience a sense of failure when couples they have counseled decide to divorce. The normal impulse is to stop relating to the couple and let them "go it alone." The couple may convey to the pastor that they want to be left alone. However, the counsel and friendship of the pastor are also urgently needed during and following the divorce experience. The stages of conflict listed by

Oates reveal divorce and postdivorce as times of deep conflict and emotional crisis. The pastor should attempt to continue functioning as a pastor even though he disagrees with the choice the couple has made.

One task for the pastor is to help the spouses eliminate unnecessary personal hurt. If either spouse chooses to cuddle treasured resentments or feelings of being dealt with unjustly, it will damage his personality. While visiting at a general hospital, I met a male patient who had divorced and remarried twenty years before. He wanted to talk about his first wife. As he spoke, his face, eyes, and hands revealed the bitter resentments he still nurtured. Apparently he had injected this same poison into his son who was also bitter toward the first wife. The patient's resentments were like cancer hurting himself, his son, his present marriage, and his relationship with God. He had not gone to church since the divorce.

A second task is to help both spouses accept their share of responsibility for the failure of their marriage. There are times when a spouse is unaware of the reason for his damaging conduct that helps wreck the marriage. He realizes vaguely he is contributing to the problem but doesn't know why. Other times a spouse feels it is entirely the fault of the companion. Likely there has never been a divorce where one spouse could wash his hands of all responsibility. Accepting a share of personal responsibility for the failure will help remove resentment and lighten the hurt experienced by children.

A husband and father suddenly left home. A note on the table was all he left behind. I had some contact with the wife and attempted to contact the husband. He did not respond. Eventually there was divorce. He remarried within a year and she about three years later.

In piecing together the story, he felt she was the total problem. She felt the same about him. Neither

106

would accept responsibility for the failure in their marriage. Both put full blame on the other.

The children frequently expressed anger and bitterness toward the father, obviously being influenced by the mother, who placed all the blame on him. They said their father married a cross-eyed Oriental. They broke an item in the home that was made by a friend of their father. These are indications the mother did not accept her share of the responsibility for the divorce, which brought additional hurt to the children.

The third major task of the pastor is to solicit the help of both spouses to minimize emotional damage to children. They are usually the innocent victims, who suffer most from the events surrounding divorce. Every year 150,000 to 200,000 children in the United States are affected by the divorce of their parents. The following quotation describes the divorce event as children experience it:

> Children whose parents divorce can adjust themselves to the altered condition of their lives, not without pain, but with a minimum of the inevitable pain and confusion, if both of their parents maintain some clearsighted sensitivity about children's needs. A child in such a situation begins to feel different from other children long before there is an actual divorce. Whether he is three or thirteen, he soon becomes aware that his parents are not getting along together as other parents do; hence his feeling of security about his home is already shaken. Also shaken is his confidence in his parents as wise grown-ups. If Mother and Father, who have always advised him what to do, are not able to resolve their own difficulties, then his world indeed seems to be falling apart. If they no longer love each other and intend to abandon one another, then perhaps they will abandon him, too. Desperately he hopes for reconciliation between his parents, so that he will not feel so frightened and lost. Some children in their terror blame themselves for the parental crisis. Perhaps all the trouble came about because they were bad; perhaps the breaking up of the home and abandonment all around is their punishment. [8]

107

Children need to discover they are still loved by both parents even though the parents no longer love each other. Often each parent attempts to instill bitterness in the children against the other parent. The children are caught in an intense inner conflict because they want to love both parents and be loved by both. But both parents are saying, "Love me and hate your father (or mother)." Both parents must cooperate to avoid the conflict that comes from being forced to take sides. The deepest hurt experienced by children appears to come from the mishandling of the divorce experience by the parents rather than from the divorce itself.

Clinebell sees the following recommendations as principles whereby parents can minimize emotional damage to children:

(1) Avoid senseless rancor which will expose the child to added trauma.

(2) Obtain counseling to deal with their own resentments, guilt feelings, rage, hurt, and grief, so that they will not attempt to use the child as a "therapist."

(3) Obtain psychotherapy, after the acute crisis has passed, to discover and resolve the inner conflicts which contributed to the disintegration of the marriage.

(4) Help the child avoid blaming himself for the parents' problems.

(5) Be honest with the child about what is happening. [9]

Authorities vary on how much parents should tell the child. Telling too much may burden the child unnecessarily. To tell too little may distort the picture and lead to confusion. The important concern is that the child not feel he is being deliberately fooled by the parents. He needs to know that Mother and Father once loved each other and that they still both love him. The concern for the well-being of the children raises many questions and the pastor should be able to provide some guidance.

A fourth task is to provide counsel during the period of emotional crisis. The emotional reactions and physical symptoms common during this crisis period were discussed in Chapter 3 and need not be repeated. It is important to remember that the pastor is probably in the best position to stand by persons in this period of need. Frequently they will not continue seeing a counselor. Their hostile attitudes make it difficult for friends to continue being friendly. Unless the pastor makes special effort to maintain contact, the divorcee may face his battles entirely alone. The pastor must be prepared for changing attitudes and unpredictable behavior but this should not stop him from attempting to fill a vitally needed role at a crucial time in the person's life. My worst tongue-lashing came from such a person. The pastor can be a needed friend one day and an unwanted enemy the next day.

The fifth task of the pastor is to help the divorcees develop new relationships. For many people divorce has meant losing a spouse, losing friends, and possibly losing a job. Many meaningful relationships have been cut. They are like an uprooted plant. If the divorcee is to come alive again, new relationships must be built. Some go to a bar. Others go to a church. Ideally, the church is the forgiving community. Here persons should rediscover the love and forgiveness of God. While the pastor cannot provide all that is needed in building new relationships, he can offer suggestions of groups and clubs where the divorcees can become reestablished in society and rebuild a circle of friends.

In summary, the pastor has the opportunity of filling a most significant role as he relates to couples in conflict. As pastor, he strongly desires to see the sick marriage regain health and wholeness. He knows the various counseling resources in his community and explains their approach to needy couples. As counselor, he knows he cannot control the life of any couple. He is a resource person presenting options when basic decisions are being made about the future of a marriage. As a shepherd, he stands by his sheep even if they choose to go through the valley of separation or divorce. He attempts to help them internalize forgiveness toward themselves and others and to practice love in circumstances of conflict.

Few tasks demand more skill, patience, and wisdom than the pastor's role as outlined in this chapter. Fulfilling this role is only possible through the strength of the Good Shepherd who gave His life for His sheep.

CHAPTER 3

Counseling Persons Considering Remarriage

The majority of divorcees remarry. Various studies indicate that about 90 percent of the people who divorce enter another marriage relationship. Therefore, this study would not be complete without dealing with the issue of remarriage.

Divorce and remarriage are two separate steps for many people. True, 90 percent remarry but we cannot say that all of these had plans for remarriage at the time of divorce.

This chapter will follow a pattern similar to the preceding one. A verbatim account of a counseling situation will be examined where the central issue focuses on remarriage. The model developed in Chapter 1 of Part II will be used to evaluate the sessions.

Then we will focus on how the pastor deals with the past, present, and future facets of the remarriage issue. Past conflicts and failures are important because they are a definite part of the present unless they have been adequately faced and resolved. The pastor must determine whether the past is actually past or whether it is a disturbing part of the present.

The present is likewise important. Specific reasons caused the past marriage to fail. Has there been sufficient growth in self-understanding and maturity that the remarriage will not repeat the failures of the first one? Do present prospects point toward the ability to build a solid marriage relation?

Remarriage assumes a future. A second marriage for

Christian couples takes them into new relationships with self, family, and church. Will they be able to live happily in these relationships? Marriage requires premarital counseling. Counseling is even more important before remarriage.

Case Study

This case is taken from *Casebook in Pastoral Counseling* edited by Cryer and Vayhinger.

A young couple knocked at the parsonage door one evening, standing first on one foot and then the other, in the age-old tip-off that they had matrimony in mind. He was in army uniform and about twenty-one. She was rather plain looking, I judged about eighteen or nineteen.

FIRST CALL

Bob: I'm Bob — and this is Jenny. We'd like to talk to you about getting married.

Jenny: Yes, I want to be married in your church because I've been to one of your weddings and you make it so nice.

Pastor: Thank you. I'll be glad to officiate at your wedding, but I would like to talk with you both about the wedding and the marriage. Have you time to talk it all over tonight?

Together: Yes; that's what we came for. (They told me he was at a post about twenty miles away, and that she works in a cafe in the town nearest the post. She at one time lived here but now was living with her parents in D————. She stressed that she wanted to be married in this church.)

Pastor: I think it very important that you be married in a church. It helps put another solid foundation under a marriage. Did you attend this church when you lived here?

Jenny: No, I never went much except to Sunday school, and that was at the church down the street. (She gestured toward the Pentecostal church.)

Pastor: Are you a member of that church now?

Jenny: No, I don't guess I am, 'cause, you see, I have to work Sundays, so I can't go.

Pastor: How about Bob? Are you a member?

Bob: No, my home is way out on a ranch, and we never went

to church when I was a kid. I sometimes go to chapel on the base (with a sheepish grin). Well, once, anyway.

Pastor: Um-hm. Well, I feel that marriage is rather like a three-legged stool, and religion is one of the legs. Leave it out and the stool will fall. Overemphasize or underemphasize it and the whole thing is out of balance. If I marry you, I would like you to join some church and become regular attending members. Would you do that?

Together (hesitantly): I guess we should.

Pastor: Another very important leg on which the marriage stands is finance. Bob, do you have enough income to support a wife?

Bob: Yes, we figure she'll work until I'm out of the service, then we'll go home to the ranch where I'll be with my dad.

Pastor: You will eventually own the ranch?

Bob: Yes.

Pastor: Jenny, do you like the idea of living on a ranch 150 miles from the city?

Jenny: Yeah, I guess so, long as I can be with Bob.

Pastor: Well, you will have to figure out your finances, but I wanted you to remember it is an important item in marriage. Where will you live for the next eight months until Bob is out of the service?

Jenny (as though surprised at the question): With my folks.

Pastor: You will have your own home, but in the same house?

Jenny: Yeah, we'll have our apartment in the basement.

Pastor: You have it ready?

Jenny: No, but it will be by the time we're married.

Pastor: Um-hm. The third leg of the stool in marriage is sex. Again, it must be kept in balance to make the marriage stand. (Their faces remained expressionless.) The good Lord made us male and female: that's why you are attracted to each other. Therefore, it is not something to be ashamed of. It is too bad that the subject has been taboo in polite conversation. I feel that it is important that you approach your marriage with as great a knowledge of the subject as you can get from others and then recognize that when it is guided by holy love it becomes a holy thing. If you'd like, I can give you a copy of *Harmony in Marriage* by Leland Wood (Round Table Press, out of print.)

Bob: I'd like that.

Pastor: I'll have it for you at the rehearsal, for we will need one. Do you want me to speak to the church organist for the service?

113

Jenny: No, I don't want her. I want Miss ———— to play.

Pastor: I think that could be arranged; she is one of our assistant organists.

Jenny: And I want ———— to sing, but I won't have time to ask them, so will you do that?

Pastor: I believe I will see them.

(We talked for about an hour, discussing the whole marriage problem and setting the date for the wedding and a rehearsal. I have, of course, merely reported the highlights of the conversation. My impression was that they were a typical young couple whose concept of marriage would develop after they got into it. He seemed the more mature of the two. When the interview seemed at an end, I suggested that I'd like to offer a prayer for the success of the marriage. They agreed readily, so I besought the Lord's guidance, somewhat as follows:)

Pastor: God our Father, we thank Thee for Thy love which is made known to us also in our love for one another. May it ever be the guiding light for Bob and Jenny as they begin sharing each other's life. Help them to keep Thee as their companion throughout both the joys and heartbreaks of married life. Hear our prayer in the name of Jesus and for our sakes. Amen.

(They departed saying, "We'll see you in church.")

About two weeks later I received replies from both the musicians that they would not be able to perform at the wedding. On the day the organist informed me she could not play, I received an invitation to the wedding, and the name of the parents of the bride-to-be was not the one Jenny had given me. I mentioned that to the organist.

Organist: Now I know who the girl is. She got married before she finished high school. When you gave me the parents' name, I placed her. What is she doing getting married again?

Pastor: This is all news to me. Neither she nor the boy said anything about a previous marriage.

Organist: Well, I know she married during her senior year in high school. She did finish the year and graduate, but she could not have been married for two years yet.

Pastor: Thank you for this information. Since you cannot play for her, I have reason to call her, and I think I shall ask some pointed questions.

Organist: I hope I haven't said anything I shouldn't.

Pastor: Indeed you haven't. Thank you for being very helpful.
(I telephoned, and failed to get either the girl or her mother. A sister-in-law answered the phone. I explained who I was and that I wanted some further information about the wedding plans.)

Sister-in-law: Perhaps I can help you.

Pastor: I have heard that Jenny has been married before. Is that correct?

Sister-in-law: I'm afraid it is.

Pastor: She seems very young for that. How long ago was the divorce granted?

Sister-in-law: About the time they came to see you.

Pastor: I would like to talk with the couple about the whole matter. I find that the musicians she wanted cannot play and sing, and I certainly want to know more about this divorce matter. Will you tell them I want to see them?

SECOND CALL

Two days later the couple appeared, the girl showing a rather defiant attitude.

Pastor: Come in.

Jenny: Mary said you wanted to see us.

Pastor: Yes, I do. I learned rather inadvertently that you are divorced. Is that true?

Jenny: Yes, but divorced people get married every day.

Pastor: Yes, I know that, but I also know that the church looks with disfavor on it and has set certain standards which we ministers must follow. Why didn't you tell me of this when you were here before?

Jenny: You didn't ask.

Pastor: Perhaps I should have, but in one as young as you, I didn't expect it. Not until I saw your parents' name as different from yours — did I even give it a thought, and then I supposed that your mother had married again. Why are you secretive about it?

Jenny (rather lamely): Well, we didn't want Bob's folks to know about it.

Pastor: Jenny, do you think that starting a second marriage on misrepresentation is a good foundation when you already had one go on the rocks? (No answer.) I am allowed, by church law, to administer the rite of matrimony to a divorced person in the case of the innocent party. Who brought suit in your case — did you?

Jenny: No, he did.

Pastor: On what grounds?

Jenny: I don't know. His mother put him up to it.

Pastor: Where was it granted?

Jenny: In ———— (another state).

Pastor: How long ago?

Jenny: Well, it was done about three weeks ago, but I haven't the money to get the papers. The lawyer told me in a letter that all I need to do is pay for them, and if I want to get married, his letter is proof of the divorce.

Pastor: You mean the divorce is not complete, and yet you propose to get married again? (I know I sounded surprised.)

Jenny: But it's all right; the lawyer says so.

Pastor: Jenny, marriage is so important a thing that society has put certain legal restrictions around it. But more than that, the church as spokesman of God regards it as a holy thing and sometimes does not extend its blessing upon it even when legal requirements are met, if the persons seem not to regard it as the holy, inviolate thing it is. You have placed me in an embarrassing position with my church. (Pause.) Having once been married, it is not in good taste that you plan a large church wedding with white gown and the usual trappings of a bride's wedding.

Jenny: (brightening): Well, I'm not going to be married in white. I've decided to wear a blue dress, ballerina length.

Pastor: What you wear is not of much consequence if you are not mentally and spiritually prepared for taking a vow which concludes "until death do us part"; and frankly, Jenny, I don't think you are ready for marriage. (She looked at me with defiance because I was denying her something that she wanted. I half expected her to stamp her foot.)

Bob: Maybe in view of all this, we'd better call the whole thing off. (I remained silent for a moment, praying for guidance.)

Jenny: Okay, let's go, we ain't gettin' anywhere here.

Pastor: I'm very sorry for all this misunderstanding, and I hope that we can help you when you are ready for marriage.

PASTOR'S COMMENTS

They left without any further word, but the determined stride on Jenny's part prevented my being very surprised when a small article appeared in the local paper to the effect that the parents announced her forthcoming marriage, but did not state where or by whom.

(1) I wonder where I failed in my first interview to uncover the immaturity of the girl.

(2) Did I rely too much on the boy's maturity that the marriage would succeed if these other complications had not prevented my marrying them?

(3) Was I too harsh and objective when I realized I had been "played for a sucker"?

(4) How much responsibility does a church have toward people who have no connection with it?

(5) I feel that this couple will always have a sour attitude toward my denomination because of this, but what could I have done differently?

(6) When the boy suggested "calling the whole thing off," should I have inquired to see if he meant break the engagement or merely to drop the church out of their plans?

o   o   o

I have some very real questions about the stand of his church on divorce. If people can be forgiven for other violations of the Sermon on the Mount, surely they can be forgiven for divorce, providing that they see it, are penitent, and are ready to grow beyond it. The approach to people who have failed in marriage needs to be made with compassion, understanding, and great patience, as it needs to be in every other kind of failure. We can add to guilt and resentment or, by the grace of our Lord, people can grow into freedom and greater excellence.[1]

The verbatim account will be evaluated from three points of view. First, from the standpoint of the model developed in Chapter 1 of Part II, the pastor failed at several major points. He did not begin the interview by listening and responding to feelings. Talking seemed to come more naturally than listening. Responding to their wishes came more readily than responding to their feelings. He agreed to marry them without first getting a picture of the situation.

Early in the interview, the pastor asked a number of questions but many of them were not essential to providing necessary information. It was not necessary for the pastor to know whether Bob would someday own the ranch. Questions about church membership, finances, and housing were important questions for premarital counseling but they came too early in the counseling session. If the early questions had focused on their courtship, their expectations in marriage, and their preparation for marriage, the outcome would likely have been much different. Only after the tip-off of divorce did the pastor ask pointed questions. The pastor failed to uncover immaturity in the first interview because he failed to deal with the most important issues at the proper time.

Pointed questions were raised in the second interview but the purpose seemed to be to place blame on Jenny for getting the pastor in an embarrassing position rather than helping the couple work through a solution to the problem. The counseling procedure did not develop to the point where they could explore alternatives together. Furthermore, the stages of guidance and spiritual support were not reached. The verbatim account is an example of an abortive experience in counseling.

A second focus of evaluation relates to the pastor's general handling of his role. Apparently he saw himself as their errand boy. Bob and Jenny personally knew the organist and soloist they wished to have assist in the service. They should have contacted them.

When the pastor called Jenny for information about her previous marriage, he should not have discussed the question with the sister-in-law. A concern of this magnitude should only have been discussed with Jenny and in person, not over the phone.

Jenny was not ready for marriage, according to the pastor. Perhaps he was correct, but the approach he used in telling her so was more harmful than helpful. If he could have helped her discover the areas where growth was

118

needed, some positive good may have resulted from the counseling even though he would have decided not to perform the ceremony.

The third focus of evaluation relates to how such a situation should be handled from the viewpoint of our theology. The pastor agreed to marry the couple even though they were total strangers to him. When he discovered neither was a church member, he asked for a promise that they would join a church if he would marry them.

Christian marriage involves a covenant between a man and a woman and between the couple and God. Chapter 1 of Part I discussed this concept as being basic to Christian marriage. A covenant of this nature is only possible when both the man and the woman know God personally through Jesus Christ. The pastor seemed to assume that church membership would guarantee the spiritual requirements for Christian marriage. Furthermore, he implied that these requirements can be met as well after marriage as before.

Mennonite theology would see Christian commitment as a necessary part of the preparation for Christian marriage. It is a basic issue the pastor should have worked through before promising to perform the ceremony.

The position of the pastor regarding remarriage was that he would marry only the innocent party. Who was the innocent party? Apparently the spouse that did not bring suit. It is difficult to support the innocent party concept. If an appeal is made to Matthew 5 or 19, the "innocent" party would be the faithful spouse and the "guilty" party would be the unfaithful one. The innocent party and guilty party are not determined by who brought suit.

In addition, as we observed earlier in the study, an unfaithful act grows out of a sick relationship and the health of the relationship involves both spouses. To assume that there can be a totally innocent party is unrealistic. All available evidence points in the direction of shared guilt. The primary concern is not whether the divorcee was innocent or guilty. Rather, the major concern is the extent to which the divorcee has dealt with the past regardless of what the past may have been.

What responsibility does the church have toward people seeking marriage who are not related to the church? The church should carry a concern for all persons, both members and nonmembers. However, this does not mean that a pastor is automatically a marrying parson. A Christian marriage is only possible for Christian people. If a couple is not interested in a Christian marriage, they can have a civil marriage. The church should not be "used" by them. If a couple is not Christian but wishes a Christian marriage, then the church should work with them leading them to faith and the necessary preparation for genuine Christian marriage. The church is the servant of Christ, not merely the servant of man.

Face Past Failures

Failure is the primary emotion of the divorcee. "Divorce represents failure," says Eickhoff, "no matter how one-sided that failure was. . . ."[2] Chapter 3 of Part I discussed the guilt of failure as a part of the price of divorce. But the sense of failure does not automatically include a sense of responsibility for that failure. And without a sense of responsibility for failure, personal forgiveness and growth will not be experienced.

Statistics indicate a higher rate of divorce among divorcees who remarry than among first-time marriages. Why? Because persons tend to repeat their mistakes unless they have learned from them.

A basic responsibility of the counselor is to discover what the divorcee has learned through the experience of divorce. If the divorcee has accepted responsibility for the failure and grown through the experience, he will be able to express where he failed and how he intends to function differently when he remarries. He will express forgiveness toward himself and also toward the spouse. After receiving counsel, a divorced wife said:

> The understanding I have gained is going to make it a lot easier for me to accept the role of a divorcee; otherwise, I should have gone through a bitter inner conflict, because at the climax of this break in our marriage I felt I was being unjustly and cruelly treated. At that time I could think of nothing specific that I had done that could have helped to precipitate the situation.

This woman was not discussing remarriage but she would more likely have had a successful remarriage than without the insight she expressed.

In the case study, Jenny wanted to keep the fact of her divorce hidden from Bob's parents. It would appear that Jenny had not faced her past failures. In fact, she wanted to enter a second marriage as if it were her first. The likelihood of her second marriage being successful was not great.

Bitterness toward the first spouse can be as damaging to the remarriage as failure to learn from past failures. The patient visited at a general hospital, referred to in Chapter 2, of Part II, had not dealt with his bitterness toward his first wife. Even though the second marriage had lasted many years, it was filled with continuing conflict.

According to Eickhoff, persons contemplating remarriage should be helped by the Christian church toward an "(1) understanding of their responsibility for the failure in the first marriage, (2) a sufficient interval to permit adjustment and full acceptance of this responsibility so that divorce will not happen again, and (3) the firm commitment of the person concerned to establish, this time, a Christian home."[3]

The pastor must make some judgment regarding the qualifications of the divorcee for remarriage. Only as these stipulations are met can he in good conscience feel the divorcee has the right to try again.

Assess Present Maturity

The church carries a unique responsibility in relationship to marriage. Why? Because 90 percent of the persons who marry prefer to have the ceremony performed by a minister. And since 90 percent of the persons who divorce remarry, the church is involved in marrying many divorcees.

Every pastor makes an important decision when he agrees to marry any couple. By this agreement, he is indicating he feels the persons have the potential for a successful marriage. To perform a ceremony when the possibility of success seems remote is to fall below the high calling of a minister of Jesus Christ. Therefore, the pastor must assess the maturity of every couple who comes to him for marriage. This is especially true when remarriage is involved.

Wayne Oates suggests the church should urge a waiting period for engaged couples to test the probable permanence of the marriage. "It would give the church and the pastor an opportunity for instruction, guidance, encouragement, and comfort to the couple in their pilgrimage toward the kind of maturity that marriage requires."[4] Without maturity successful marriage is unlikely.

Chapter 2 of Part I focused on requirements for successful marriage. The key requirement was the ability to relate in depth. This requires openness, caring, and trust. True, these are intangible qualities, but their presence or absence can be detected by observing how the couple relates. In premarital counseling, the pastor should attempt to determine the nature of their interpersonal relationships.

A neurotic pattern in one or both spouses is the cause for many marriage failures. Studies by Bergler supporting this thesis were examined in Chapter 3 of Part I. Passing through a divorce court does not heal a neurotic. Repeated marriages will likely result in failure. "Good intentions are not sufficient to overcome neurotic drives that compel people to do things which common sense would clearly forbid."[5] If neurotic patterns are evident, the major need is professional counseling, not marriage.

One common expression of immaturity is sexual unfaithfulness. Wynn says that the person who cheats at sex is immature and needs to grow up. If sexual cheating was involved in ending the previous marriage, the pastor can be reasonably sure he is dealing with an immature person unless there is evidence that growth has taken place.

Assessing present maturity may not be easy but it is important. If the pastor concludes the marriage will not likely succeed, he will need to be open and direct in helping the couple face their real situation. The answer may be no marriage, a postponed marriage, or their decision to be married by some other person. They must work this out together. But the pastor will have been faithful to his responsibility under God.

Examine Future Implications

Marriage is for the future. For the couple the present moment seems the most important and the honeymoon the immediate dream. But marriage vows are for "as long as we both shall live." And the living of the vows for the Christian couple involves a relationship with self, family, and church. Can the couple face these relationships with confidence?

The remarried person must be able to live with himself. The way he views remarriage will help to mold the nature of that marriage. Some persons would have a disturbing sense of guilt if they were to remarry while the former partner is still living. Loneliness may motivate them toward marriage and the guilt may be suppressed temporarily. But after the newness of marriage is past, the sense of guilt returns and the person has difficulty living with himself and with the spouse. The marriage relation will be strained and growth will not take place.

The pastor should be direct in working through this question with the divorcee. The convictions of the pastor cannot be forced on the person seeking remarriage. He must be persuaded in his own mind. Emerson describes this persuasion in clear terms.

> This concept of being married "in the Lord" means that there is one considered, ultimate authority in the decision to remarry. That is the authority that comes not from the minister or from the law of the church or land, nor from the desires of the couple. It is the authority of a revelation that breaks through the counseling situation into the presence of the parties concerned. I have defined it as the point of "readiness for marriage."[6]

The sense of "readiness for marriage" may not come in the same way Emerson describes but it should be a clear conviction in the mind of the divorcee.

Marriage also involves the relationship of family. In a certain deep sense, marriage involves the families of the couple. One does not marry a family but he does marry into a family. The pastor should inquire concerning the feelings of the families involved. Will they accept the new family member?

Another facet of the picture concerns the attitude of the members of the original family of the divorced person. Their attitude is especially important where children are involved. Will the marriage cut off the children from important family relationships? Generally the original family approves a remarriage if they feel it has the possibility of being a happy marriage.

Children of the divorcee considering remarriage should also be considered. If they still love the other parent, usually the father, they may see a "new father" as an intruder. If a new family is to be established where children are involved, it is important to be sure that they will be involved by accepting the new parent.

Three separate family relationships have been mentioned. All are important. If there are difficulties involving certain of these relationships, it does not mean that the marriage should not take place. But the pastor should help both parties enter marriage with their eyes open, aware of what relationships they will likely encounter in marriage.

In addition to self and family, marriage also involves the church. Since the marriage covenant is seen as relating to community, Christian marriage should be a congregational experience. The witnesses to the marriage should include some who will worship with them after marriage. Acceptance by the congregation is most important where there has been remarriage. Members of a congregation who do not feel acceptance will not become a vital part of the fellowship.

Certain congregations require a vote of the membership before receiving persons involved in divorce and remarriage. The reason is that membership without acceptance has no meaning or personal value. The following letter illustrates the importance of the attitude of the congregation:

Dear Pastor,

I am writing to ask for help. I had an unsuccessful first marriage that ended in divorce. After several years, I met a man who has become my husband. He is a most wonderful person. We have had a good marriage for the last three years, and I have every reason to believe that it will continue to be. But one of the big problems we face is the attitude of the people in our church. The members of the congregation glare at us. I have spoken to the minister. Even he is confused. What does the church have to say to us?

This lady had been remarried in the church but not accepted by the church. A vote by the membership of the congregation before remarriage may also help prevent the tragedy of a marriage not accepted by the congregation.

Eickhoff expresses well the attitude of an accepting congregation when he says that "the church members must be readied to accept divorced persons and those remarried in the church as repentant sinners who deserve a second chance and the support of the community in Christian love."[7]

Premarital counseling should include exploring the three areas of relationships discussed above because of their implications for the future of the marriage.

The scope of counseling outlined in this chapter is broad and time-consuming. However, if the result is a successful remarriage, the time spent is a good investment. Few tragedies are as great as a broken marriage and few successes greater than a truly satisfying marriage relationship. Successful remarriage involves much more than a correct understanding of biblical doctrine, as important as that is; it involves spiritual and emotional maturity. The pastor has the unique responsibility of helping the couple discover whether they possess these qualifications.

CHAPTER 4

Conclusion

This book was written to help the pastor with convictions concerning the permanence of marriage discover how to counsel more effectively persons considering divorce or remarriage.

I have assumed in this book that the traditional approach of such a pastor has proved inadequate to meet the needs of persons caught in problem marriages and divorce. I have suggested that a solution could be found based on both the biblical view of marriage and the dynamics of the particular situation involved. On the basis of my study I have proposed that persons involved in divorce and remarriage may be received as church members on an individual basis when there is evidence of faith and forgiveness.

A significant number of findings support the thesis of this book. In the Old Testament, resuming a marriage following a second marriage was strictly forbidden. This advice was a part of the traditional approach of the Mennonite Church after it returned to a rigid position around 1900.

Matthew 5 and 19 give impenitent unfaithfulness as grounds for divorce and remarriage. 1 Corinthians 7 allows irremedial desertion as a valid ground for terminating a marriage. The New Testament seems to view adultery as an act rather than a state.

Of the four attitudes of the Christian church toward divorce and remarriage listed by Oates, the laissez-faire approach and the forensic approach have elements similar to the approach of the Mennonite Church from 1900 to 1950. The confrontational and therapeutic approach is closer to that of the sixteenth-century Anabaptists and the Mennonite Church at the close of the nineteenth century.

One's understanding of marriage determines his approach to divorce and remarriage. If the essence of marriage is sexual union, divorce and remarriage are permissible only when there has been adultery. When marriage is seen in terms of covenant, breaking the marriage is always sin. Seeing marriage only in terms of the relationship between two persons allows for breaking one relationship and starting another without sin. In Christian marriage, however, all three aspects are involved and are vitally significant.

The Anabaptists allowed divorce in case of adultery and desertion, and remarriage in case of adultery. From 1867 to 1900, the Mennonite Church allowed remarriage when divorce was due to adultery, and church membership for remarried persons if they repented of their sin.

These findings support the thesis of this book and provide guidance for an alternative to the traditional viewpoint which allowed no remarriage or church membership for remarried persons. The alternative is seen in the answer to the basic question of how a Mennonite pastor counsels persons considering divorce or remarriage.

According to the model for counseling, the pastor's role is both careful listening and aggressive action. His approach is not client-centered but person-centered. The pastor is both a strong and loving person. His role is basically the confrontational and therapeutic approach. He understands marriage in terms of sexual union, covenant, and personal relationships.

When counseling with spouses in a disturbed marriage, the pastor is aware of both the external and internal forces that are destroying marriage and is alert to detect their presence. He is aware of the requirement of building a satisfying relationship in order to have a successful marriage and works to help relationships grow.

CONCLUSION

If the marital conflicts cannot be corrected, he sees separation as the scriptural answer although this involves failure to keep covenant and falls below God's intention.

When counseling with persons considering divorce, the pastor helps them see the implication of breaking covenant. He helps them become aware of the emotional cost of divorce and the futility of divorce where neurotic patterns are involved. He assesses the marriage attempting to locate the basic conflicts. He explores the options of professional counseling, trial separation, annulment if appropriate, and divorce. Finally, the couple must decide on their course of action. If the choice is divorce, the pastor attempts to provide pastoral care during and following the painful divorce experience.

When counseling persons interested in remarriage, the pastor attempts to help them face their past failures. The purpose is not to establish guilt or innocence but to see whether the divorcees have honestly faced their part in the marriage failure and grown through the experience. The pastor needs to assess their present maturity to determine whether there is a high degree of likelihood that the marriage will succeed. Together they examine the future implications of the marriage for themselves, their families, and their relationship to their church. After counseling in these areas, the couple needs to decide whether God is in fact leading them to take the step of marriage.

Few tasks demand more of the pastor than working with persons in conflicting marital situations. But his job is made more difficult if he is uncertain what his role should be and how he should function. On the other hand, his task is less difficult if he is clear on what he should attempt to do. This book has attempted to help bring clarity to the pastor as he counsels persons considering divorce or remarriage.

Notes

PART I

CHAPTER 1

1. J. C. Wenger, *Dealing Redemptively with Those Involved in Divorce and Remarriage Problems* (Scottdale, Pa.: Herald Press, 1965), p. 9.
2. William Graham Cole, *Sex and Love in the Bible* (New York: Association Press, 1959), p. 332.
3. *Ibid.*, p. 335.
4. Wenger, *op. cit.*, p. 12.
5. *Ibid.*, p. 23.
6. Howard H. Charles, "Some Aspects of the New Testament Teaching on Divorce and Remarriage." Study paper presented at Indiana-Michigan Mennonite Conference, Goshen, Indiana, 1955.
7. Otto A. Piper, *The Biblical View of Sex and Marriage* (New York: Charles Scribner's Sons, 1960), p. 29.
8. G. Ernest Wright, *The Biblical Doctrine of Man in Society*, Ecumenical Biblical Studies No. 2 (London SCM Press, LTD, 1954), p. 24.
9. *Ibid.*, p. 25.
10. *Love and Conflict*, p. 83, copyright © 1958 by Gibson Winter. Reprinted by permission of Doubleday & Company, Inc.
11. Alvin Toffler, *Future Shock* (New York: Random House, 1970), p. 217.
12. *The Complete Writings of Menno Simons*, trans. by Leonard Verduin and ed. by J. C. Wenger (Scottdale, Pa.: Herald Press, 1956), p. 200.
13. Wenger, *op. cit.*, pp. 15, 16.

CHAPTER 2

1. Maxwell S. Stewart, ed., *Problems of Family Life* (New York: Harper & Brothers Publishers, 1946), pp. 140, 141.
2. F. Alexander Magoun, *Love and Marriage* (New York: Harper and Bros., 1956), p. 171.
3. William J. Lederer and Don D. Jackson, *The Mirages of Marriage* (New York: W. W. Norton & Company, Inc., 1968), p. 56.
4. Clemens E. Benda, "Divorce from a Psychiatrist's Point of View," *Pastoral Psychology*, September 1958, p. 37.
5. Lederer and Jackson, *op. cit.*, p. 56.
6. *Ibid.*, p. 78.
7. John F. Cuber with Peggy B. Harroff, *The Significant Americans* (New York: Appleton-Century, 1965), pp. 44-60.
8. Winter, *op. cit.*, p. 25.
9. Howard J. Clinebell, Jr., and Charlotte H. Clinebell, *The Intimate Marriage* (New York, Evanston, and London: Harper & Row, Publishers, 1970), p. 25.
10. *Ibid.*, p. 68.
11. *Ibid.*, p. 75.
12. *Ibid.*, p. 69.

NOTES

CHAPTER 3

1. Morton M. Hunt, *The World of the Formerly Married* (New York, Toronto, London, Sydney: McGraw-Hill Book Company, 1966), pp. 3, 4. Used with permission.

2. William J. Goode, *After Divorce* (Glencoe, Illinois: The Free Press, 1956), p. 188. Used by permission of Macmillan Publishing Company, Inc.

3. Nancy Love, "Everything You Always Wanted to Know About Divorce (But Were Afraid to Ask)," *Philadelphia Magazine*, September 1970, p. 71.

4. James H. Burns, "What It Means to Be Divorced," *Pastoral Psychology*, September 1958, p. 46.

5. James G. Emerson, "The Church and the Divorced Woman," *Pastoral Psychology*, December 1967, p. 23.

6. Burns, *op. cit.*, p. 46.

7. *Ibid.*, p. 45.

8. Goode, *op. cit.*, p. 331.

9. Edmund Bergler, *Divorce Won't Help* (New York, Evanston, and London: Harper & Row, Publishers, 1948), p. 7.

10. *Ibid.*, p. 23.

11. Stewart, *op. cit.*, p. 122.

PART II

CHAPTER 1

1. Niebuhr and Williams, editors, *The Ministry in Historical Perspective* (New York: Harper & Row).

2. From *Pastoral Counseling* by Seward Hiltner, p. 95. Copyright 1949 by Pierce & Smith (Abingdon Press).

3. From *Basic Types of Pastoral Counseling* by Howard J. Clinebell, Jr., p. 28. Copyright © 1966 by Abingdon Press.

4. *Ibid.*, p. 30.

5. Quoted from Clinebell, *Basic Types of Pastoral Counseling*, p. 39.

6. *Ibid.*, pp. 27, 28.

7. Richard K. Young in Oates, *op. cit.*, p. 119.

8. *Ibid.*, p. 112.

9. *Ibid.*, p. 114.

10. Clinebell, *op. cit.*, pp. 91, 92.

11. Paul E. Johnson, *Psychology of Pastoral Care* (New York, Nashville: Abingdon Press, 1953), p. 145.

12. Clinebell, *op. cit.*, pp. 101, 102.

CHAPTER 2

1. From *Casebook in Pastoral Counseling* edited by Newman S. Cryer and John M. Vayhinger, pp. 103-107. Copyright © 1962 by Abingdon Press.

2. From *Pastoral Ministry to Families* by John Charles Wynn, p. 141. Copyright, MCMLVII, by W. L. Jenkins. Used with permission of The Westminster Press.

3. Samuel Southard in *An Introduction to Pastoral Counseling*, Wayne E. Oates, ed. (Nashville: Broadman Press, 1959), pp. 165-167. Used by permission.

4. David R. Mace, "The Pastor and Divorce," *Pastoral Psychology*, September 1958, p. 9.

5. Cuber with Harroff, *op. cit.*, p. 90.

6. Wynn, *op. cit.*, p. 152.

7. Goode, *op. cit.*, p. 173.

8. Phillip Polatin and Ellen C. Philtine, "Children and Divorce," *Pastoral Psychology*, October 1958, p. 34.

9. Clinebell, *op. cit.*, pp. 202, 203.

CHAPTER 3

1. Cryer and Vayhinger, *op. cit.*, pp. 77-81.

2. Andrew R. Eickhoff, *A Christian View of Sex and Marriage* (New York: The Free Press, 1966) p. 211.

3. Eickhoff, *op. cit.*, p. 212.

4. Oates, *op. cit.*, p. 106.

5. John Sutherland Bonnell, "Counseling with Divorced Persons," *Pastoral Psychology*, September 1958, p. 15.

6. James G. Emerson, Jr., *Divorce, the Church, and Remarriage* (Philadelphia: The Westminster Press, 1961), pp. 171, 172.

7. Eickhoff, *op. cit.*, p. 212.

Bibliography

Aldrich, C. Knight and Nighswonger, Carl. *A Pastoral Counseling Casebook.* Philadelphia: The Westminster Press, 1968.

Bainton, Roland H. *What Christianity Says About Sex, Love and Marriage.* New York: Association Press, 1957.

Bergler, Edmund. *Divorce Won't Help.* New York: Hart Publishing Company, Inc., 1948.

Clinebell, Howard J., Jr. *Basic Types of Pastoral Counseling.* Nashville, New York: Abingdon Press, 1969.

―――. and Clinebell, Charlotte H. *The Intimate Marriage.* New York: Harper and Row, Publishers, 1970.

Cole, William Graham. *Sex and Love in the Bible.* New York: Association Press, 1959.

Cryer, Newman S., Jr., and Vayhinger, John Monroe. *Casebook in Pastoral Counseling.* New York, Nashville: Abingdon Press, 1962.

Cuber, John F. with Harroff, Peggy B. *The Significant Americans.* New York: Appleton-Century, 1965.

Eickhoff, Andrew R. *A Christian View of Sex and Marriage.* New York: The Free Press, 1966.

Emerson, James G., Jr. *Divorce, the Church and Remarriage.* Philadelphia: The Westminster Press, 1961.

Goode, William J. *After Divorce.* Glencoe, Illinois: The Free Press, 1956.

Hiltner, Seward. *Pastoral Counseling.* New York, Nashville: Abingdon Press, 1949.

Hunt, Morton M. *The World of the Formerly Married.* New York, Toronto, London, Sydney: McGraw-Hill Book Company, 1966.

Johnson, Paul E. *Psychology of Pastoral Care.* New York, Nashville: Abingdon Press, 1953.

BIBLIOGRAPHY

Lederer, William J., and Jackson, Don R. *The Mirages of Marriage*. New York: W. N. Norton and Company, Inc., 1968.

Mace, David R. *Success in Marriage*. New York, Nashville: Abingdon Press, 1958.

Magoun, F. Alexander. *Love and Marriage*. New York: Harper and Bros., 1956.

Maxwell, Stewart S. ed. *Problems of Family Life*. New York: Harper and Bros., 1956.

Mudd, Emily H.; Stone, Abraham; Karpf, Maurice J.; Nelson, Janet Fowler. *Marriage Counseling: A Casebook*. New York: Association Press, 1959.

Oates, Wayne E. ed. *An Introduction to Pastoral Counseling*. Nashville: Broadman Press, 1959.

————. *Pastoral Counseling in Social Problems*. Philadelphia: The Westminster Press, 1966.

————. *Protestant Pastoral Counseling*. Philadelphia: The Westminster Press, 1962.

Piper, Otto A. *The Biblical View of Sex and Marriage*. New York: Charles Scribner's Sons, 1960.

Stewart, Charles William. *The Minister as Marriage Counselor*. New York, Nashville: Abingdon Press, 1961.

The Complete Writings of Menno Simons. trans. by Leonard Verduin and ed. by John Christian Wenger. Scottdale.: Herald Press, 1956.

The Mennonite Encyclopedia. Vol. III. Scottdale, Pa.: Mennonite Publishing House, 1957.

Thielicke, Helmut. *The Ethics of Sex*, trans, by John W. Doberstein. New York, Evanston and London: Harper and Row, 1964.

Toffler, Alvin. *Future Shock*. New York: Random House, 1970.

Wenger, John C. *Dealing Redemptively with Those Involved in Divorce and Remarriage Problems*. Scottdale, Pa.: Herald Press, 1965.

Winter, Gibson. *Love and Conflict*. New York: Dolphin Books, 1958.

Wright, G. Ernest. *The Biblical Doctrine of Man in Society*. Ecumenical Biblical Studies No. 2. London: SCM Press LTD, 1954.

Wynn, John Charles, *Pastoral Ministry to Families*. Philadelphia: The Westminster Press, 1957.

Articles

Areakian, Spurgeon. "Divorce — California Style." *Presbyterian Life,* June 1970.

Benda, Clemens E. "Divorce from a Psychiatrist's Point of View." *Pastoral Psychology,* September 1958.

Burch, I.A. "The Conciliation Counseling Service of the Divorce Division of the Circuit Court of Cook County, Illinois." *First Annual Report,* 1965 — 1966.

Charles, Howard H. "Some Aspects of the New Testament Teaching on Divorce and Remarriage." Study paper presented at Indiana-Michigan Mennonite Conference, Goshen, Indiana, 1955.

Emerson, James G., Jr. "The Church and the Divorced Woman." *Pastoral Psychology,* December 1967.

Love, Nancy, "Everything You Always Wanted to Know About Divorce (But Were Afraid to Ask)."*Philadelphia Magazine,* September 1970.

Mace, David R. "The Pastor and Divorce." *Pastoral Psychology,* September 1958.

Polatin, Phillip, and Philtine, Ellen C. "Children and Divorce." *Pastoral Psychology,* October 1958.

Wynn, J. C. "Making Marriage More Stable." *Presbyterian Life,* March 15, 1967.

Index

Adultery, 20, 22, 25, 35, 38, 123
Anabaptists, 37, 128
Astley, M. R. C., 41
Attitudes, social, 95, 97, 98

Benda, Clemens E., 50
Bergler, Edmund, 65, 122
Boisen, Anton T., 75
Bucer, Martin, 74
Burns, James H., 62
Bushnell, Horace, 75

Character disorder, 42, 96
Charles, Howard H., 22, 23
Church, relationships to, 8, 26, 31,
  99, 109, 113, 117, 123, 125
Clinebell, Howard J., Jr., 54, 55, 76,
  77, 81, 85, 100, 108
Cole, William, 18, 20
Commitment, 28, 31, 38, 55
Conflicts, inner, 66
Conscience, 23, 103
Counseling
  authority of counselor, 93-96
  basic elements, 81-83, 85
  client-centered, 76, 128
  community agencies, 67, 68, 101
  confrontational approach, 79, 80,
    82, 118, 120, 123, 124
  exploring past, 79
  failures, 105, 117, 118
  future orientation, 78, 79
  history of, 74, 75, 78
  insight-oriented, 76, 79, 121
  listening, 77, 81, 93, 95, 117
  mechanics of, 81-86
  pastoral tasks, 28, 57, 105-108, 117,
    122, 128
  person-centered, 77, 128
  premarital, 34, 112, 123, 126
  preventive, 100
  professional, 67-69, 98, 102, 123
  reconciliation, 104, 109
  relationship-centered, 77, 86
  Scripture, use of, 83, 104, 105
  short-term, 78, 81
  supportive, 79
Cryer, Newman S., Jr., 87, 112
Cuber, John F., 51, 65, 100

Divorce
  alimony, 98, 104
  attitudes of church, 24-28, 35-40,
    115, 116
  biblical view, O.T., 17-20
  biblical view, N.T., 19-24
  children, consideration of, 64, 91,
    98, 104-108
  children, custody of, 60, 98, 104
  emotional divorce, 38, 56
  emotional cost, 60-64, 69, 98, 105-
    108, 120
  emotional problems, 39, 61-63
  exception clause, 20, 21, 26, 37
  futility of, 65-69, 105
  grief, 62, 98
  grounds for, 36, 37, 41, 42
  guilty party, 26, 27, 30, 38, 46, 119
  innocent party, 21, 23, 26, 27, 30,
    36, 38, 46, 119
  identity crisis, 63, 69
  statistics, 41, 64, 96, 107, 111, 120,
    122
  physical symptoms, 63
  trauma, 59-61, 65, 98, 107, 108
Duvall, Evelyn, 42, 67, 96
Duvall, Sylvanus, 42, 67, 96

Edwards, Jonathan, 75
Eickhoff, Andrew R., 120, 126
Emerson, James G., 124
Emotional maturity, 55, 80, 111
External social patterns, 42-46

Family
  communal, 32
  courts, 68
  finances, 44, 88-92, 96, 113
  functioning, 42, 45
  husband, role of, 45
  relationships, 42, 43, 121
  roles, 80, 97, 124
  wife, role of, 45
Feelings, 77, 93
Forgiveness, 23, 27, 36, 39, 109, 120
Freud, Sigmund, 51, 66

Gladden, Washington, 75
Goode, William J., 60, 62, 65, 104
Guilt, 27, 28, 61, 62, 84, 96, 124

Healing, 28, 67-69, 78, 79
Harroff, Peggy B., 51, 65, 100
Hiltner, Seward, 75, 76
Home, importance of, 44, 65
Hunt, Morton M., 59, 60

Internal attitudes, 29, 42, 46-50
Interpersonal relationships, 44, 57, 67,
  78, 79, 84, 109

Jackson, Don R., 46
Johnson, Paul E., 83

Kauffman, Daniel, 37
Kuether, Frederick C., 75

Lederer, William J., 46
Loneliness, 47, 49, 51, 61, 97, 98
Love, 43, 46, 47, 55
Love, Nancy, 61
Luther, Martin, 74

Mace, David R., 99
Magoun, F. A., 42
Marriage
  acceptance, 54-57, 95
  adjustment, 45
  alienation, 52, 58
  annulment, 46, 104
  as covenant, 30-32
  as relationship, 32-34
  as sexual union, 29, 30, 32
  biblical view, O.T., 29
  biblical view, N.T., 23, 30, 35
  caring, 48, 54
  Christian, 26, 38, 119-121
  communication, 56, 85, 93, 97
  compatibility, 32
  conflicts, 95-99
  covenant, 27, 30-34, 38, 97, 102, 104, 119, 125
  desertion, 22, 45
  distress signals, 46, 83, 84
  growth, 54, 83-85
  hostility, 44, 45, 49, 52, 62, 84, 98, 105
  illusions, 48, 49
  incompatibility, 22, 38, 42, 96
  interaction, 53, 85
  intimacy, 51, 53, 56-58
  listening, 81, 93, 117
  need satisfaction, 48, 55, 86
  patterns of relationships, 52, 53
  permanence, 7, 23, 31, 36, 127
  religious history, 45
  romantic love, 43, 46, 48
  security, 44, 47, 56, 57, 95
  sex, 30, 33, 95, 113, 123
  spiritual resources, 83, 119
  temporary, 33
  trust, 55
  vows, 30-33, 123
Maturity, 28, 118, 122, 126
Meiburg, Albert L., 74
Model of pastoral counseling, 77-79

Needs, personality, 47, 51, 55, 56
Neurosis; neurotic patterns, 42, 65, 66, 96, 122

Oates, Wayne E., 24, 74, 81, 82, 97, 99, 106, 122

Piper, Otto A., 29
Prayer, 83, 90, 114
Presenting problem, 81, 82, 93
Psychiatrist, 101
Psychosomatic problems, 63, 69, 106
Psychotherapy, 76, 78-80, 108

Relationship development, 28, 34, 38, 49-51, 54, 68, 78, 86, 109
Remarriage, 111-126
  attitudes of church, 24-40, 112, 121, 125
  attitudes of family, 124, 125
  biblical view, O.T., 18-20
  biblical view, N.T., 19-23, 39
  congregational acceptance, 125
  counseling, 120-126
  exception clause, 21, 26
  forensic approach, 26, 27
  idealistic approach, 25, 26
  laissez-faire approach, 24, 25
  relational approach, 32, 33
  therapeutic approach, 27, 28
Responsibility, acceptance of, 39, 49, 79, 80, 85, 94, 106
Rimmer, Robert, 32
Rogers, Carl R., 76

Salter, Leslie B., 55
Self-acceptance, 95, 124
Self-confrontation, 50, 106
Self-forgiveness, 124
Self-understanding, 50, 63, 76, 111
Separation, 22, 23, 36-39, 60, 104
Sexual activity, 42, 43, 97, 123
Sexual union, 29, 32, 33, 128
Simons, Menno, 29, 34, 35
Social patterns, 43, 44
Sullivan, Harry Stock, 47

Terman, Lewis M., 41
Thielicke, Helmut, 20
Toffler, Alvin, 32

Understanding, empathic, 53-55, 81

Values, 42, 79, 80
Vayhinger, John Monroe, 87, 112

Wenger, John C., 9, 18, 21-23, 36
Winter, Gibson, 31, 54
Wright, G. Ernest, 30, 31
Wynn, John Charles, 95, 123

135

The Author

John R. Martin is Assistant Professor of Church Studies at Eastern Mennonite College, Harrisonburg, Va.

He received the BA degree from Eastern Mennonite College in 1954. From Goshen Biblical Seminary, he received the ThB in 1955 and the BD in 1960. In 1971 he completed the first unit of Clinical Pastoral Education at Lancaster General Hospital, Lancaster, Pa. He earned the ThM from The Eastern Baptist Theological Seminary in 1972.

During early seminary studies, he served as a mission pastor at Walkerton, Ind. This was followed by a three-year pastorate in a mission congregation in Washington, D.C. From 1961 to 1971, he pastored the Neffsville Mennonite Church, Neffsville, Pa. During most of this time, he also served as an area overseer in his conference district.

Other assignments have included serving as associate executive secretary of the National Service Board for Religious Objectors, Washington, D.C., director of I-W services for Mennonite Board of Missions, Elkhart, Ind., and on the Board of Trustees of Eastern Mennonite College. Currently he is president of Mennonite Broadcasts, Inc., Harrisonburg, Va.

A native of Harrisonburg, he was sixth in a closely knit family of nine children. He married Marian Landis of Blooming Glen, Pa., in 1956. The Martins have three children.